Endorsements

Andrina Rijken's "This Wondrous Life" is a book that you will want to re-read and revisit. As I read, I found myself wanting to take my time as there were so many truths that ministered to me and my personal situation. Andrina is able to draw fresh insight from scripture and apply it honestly and openly to her life. Her message is timely and extremely important - a message for generations. I hope this book is the first of many as I can hear the heart of God and the Holy Spirit speaking through her.

—Catherine Dokmanovic
—Education Manager, Consultant

In a world that is so often driving humanity to constantly achieve, strive, compare and compete 'This Wondrous Life' points the reader back to the still, small voice; to the seemingly mundane or ordinary but when lived abiding with God ultimately is extraordinary. Andrina openly invites the reader into her story providing immense encouragement through her own lived experiences and practical examples of seeing even the smallest details in life through God's Word. If you want to be encouraged in living a righteous, disciplined and truly wondrous life abiding in His presence daily then this book is for you.

—Amy Jorgensen
Director, The Extraordinary Initiative

This Wondrous Life

**Discovering the Extraordinary
Whilst Living a Seemingly Ordinary Life**

Andrina E. Rijken

Ark House Press
arkhousepress.com

© 2021 Andrina E. Rijken

All rights reserved. Apart from any fair dealing for the purpose of study, research, criticism, or review, as permitted under the Copyright Act, no part may be reproduced by any process without written permission.

Unless otherwise stated, all Scriptures are taken from the New International Translation (Holy Bible. Copyright© 1996, 2004, 2007, 2013 by Tyndale House Foundation. Used by permission of Tyndale House Publishers Inc., Carol Stream, Illinois 60188. All rights reserved.)

Some names and identifying details have been changed to protect the privacy of individuals.

Cataloguing in Publication Data:
Title: This Wondrous Life
ISBN: 978-0-6453220-2-6 (pbk)
Subjects: Christian Living
Other Authors/Contributors: Rijken, Andrina E.

Design by initiateagency.com

Dedication

To my husband, Andrew

Your love is my strength, my laughter and my song

Song of Songs 8:6-7a
*⁶ Place me like a seal over your heart,
like a seal on your arm.
For love is as strong as death,
its jealousy as enduring as the grave.
Love flashes like fire,
the brightest kind of flame.
⁷ Many waters cannot quench love,
nor can rivers drown it.*

Acknowledgements

My husband, Andrew: Thank you for championing me every step of the way. For always saying, "You can!" when I thought I couldn't. For always believing in me, and never allowing me to think I could achieve anything less. I was gifted with the best when God brought you into my life!

My children Elaina, Jet and Gip: Your love and support means the world to me. This book is a legacy for you. May you treasure it always.

Dad and Mum: Words cannot express my gratitude for all you have done for me. The sacrifices you made to ensure I always had the best opportunities never went unnoticed. Your incredible support and encouragement on this journey has been so precious to me. Mum, thank you for reading and re-reading my manuscript many times over.

Cath: My surrogate aunty - you have been one of my biggest cheerleaders in life! Having you on this journey to read parts of the book and encourage me to keep going was such a blessing.

Contents

Dedication v
Acknowledgements.. vii
Introduction... xi

Chapter 1	My Story... 1
Chapter 2	Fog 11
Chapter 3	The Better Thing... 22
Chapter 4	The Beautiful Exchange.................................... 30
Chapter 5	Wonder Woman 36
Chapter 6	My Tree Obsession 54
Chapter 7	The Naomi Phenomenon 61
Chapter 8	Dealing With Disappointment 75
Chapter 9	Laughing At the Future Part 1: Delighting in His Word... 94
Chapter 10	Laughing At the Future Part 2: Today's Laughter Is Tomorrow's Joy 106

Conclusion - This Wondrous Life!....................................... 119
Bibliography... 123
About the Author.. 125

Introduction

Have you ever wondered what it's like to be 'that girl'? You know 'that girl'– the one who everyone wants to be. The beautiful, perfectly formed bombshell, people falling at your feet, life of the party kind of girl?

Yeah, you and me both.

I'm not her.

I'm the other kind of girl.

You know the one who never does anything wrong. The 'good girl'. The 'non-rule breaker'. The one who always walks the line and checks every single box.

Every.

Single.

Time.

BORING right? Well, that's me. I'm the good girl. I've never done anything really bad or even been rebellious. The most rebellious thing I've ever done is got a second piercing in my ears. I know shocking, right? I've always toed the line and jumped through every hoop. In fact, I'm so good at hoop-jumping that I think I could be a very entertaining circus act. But realistically, who wants to see a girl jumping through hoops and doing it perfectly every time? Boring right? Yeah, we're back to that. 'Little Miss Perfect' equates to 'Little Miss Boring'!

So now I'm 44, and I'm looking back at it all and wondering what the point of always being perfect was? I've never drunk alcohol, never done drugs, never been clubbing, and I never slept around – no real past or skeletons in the closet. Yet, sometimes I think about throwing it all in and walking away from all I believe and doing something stupid, just once. Okay, who am I kidding? Thoughts like that seldomly pop in my head. Maybe when I'm having a bad day, but for only like a second, and then I feel physically ill. In all honesty, I can't fathom being like that. It's just not me. So, in keeping with the times of being who you are and expressing yourself freely, this is me. I'm that girl – the good girl, the super boring, do everything right girl, who frankly is never going to change.

I'm the girl who only had one boyfriend, and I married him. He's the love of my life, and no one on the earth has ever made me feel the way he makes me feel. I'm a mum with beautiful children who are all (surprise, surprise) good kids.

Career-wise, it's pretty run of the mill too. I went to university, worked jolly hard, nailed it, and got a degree in Speech Pathology. I've been working hard at that ever since – helping people and loving it. It's not ground-breaking – hit it out of the park, making billions kind of stuff. It's just helping people, but it's my thing.

So by now, you should be sold on this 'good girl, boring thing'. To the world, I am one giant snooze fest, right? Yep, shut the book right now cos this will be like one of those B grade sappy movies? Or maybe you're a little intrigued to read on and see how this is going to end. Is this going to be one of those teen rom-coms where the nerdy girl with glasses (yes, I wear glasses and have since a young age) turns into a supermodel, extroverted, prom queen type and gets the hot, sporty guy? Yes, I unashamedly love those movies, but this isn't going to be one of them. It is my story, though – and my story is about a girl who isn't particularly remarkable at all. She's a regular girl – a girl who's loved God all her life. That's what my story is about – loving God – loving Him every single day because, for a regular, boring, good girl like me, there is something extraordinary in that.

It's about loving Him even though life isn't always unicorns and rainbows. It's about knowing His love through the ups and downs, highs and lows. Through the dark, bucket loads of tears days, the fantastic celebrations, wars waged, and victories won days. The reality is, even the most boring of people have roller-coaster lives.

I've had moments worthy of sharing on social media, so everyone thinks I'm the bomb. But, then moments I would rather forget ever happened. The throwing yourself on the floor, crying hysterically moments where I've ended up curled in the foetal position, looking uglier than you could imagine, wondering what is the point of working hard when none of it seems to matter? And it's those moments that have led me to this – writing. Writing about me, and my seemingly regular life. About getting through the day-to-day, mundane nothingness. About learning to be content in all things and finding joy, because God is doing something incredibly beautiful in my seemingly BORING life.

I know this because He talks about girls (and guys), like me in His Word. Psalm 1 talks about BORING people like me, but God doesn't call it boring. He calls it 'the one who follows God's ways'. This is what it says:

PSALM 1 (TPT):

What delight comes to the one who follows God's ways! He won't walk in step with the wicked, nor share the sinner's way, nor be found sitting in the scorner's seat. His pleasure and passion is remaining true to the Word of "I Am," meditating day and night in the true revelation of light. He will be standing firm like a flourishing tree planted by God's design, deeply rooted by the brooks of bliss, bearing fruit in every season of his life. He is never dry, never fainting, ever blessed, ever prosperous. But how different are the wicked. All they are is dust in the wind – driven away to destruction! The wicked will not endure the Day of Judgment, for God will not defend them. Nothing they do will succeed or endure for long, for they have no part with those who walk in truth. But how different it is for the righteous! The Lord embraces their paths as they move forward while the way of the wicked leads only to doom.

More about Psalm 1 later, but let's just say I'm one of those Christians that Psalm 1 is talking about.

I was pretty much born saved (well, not quite – I'll tell you that story later too), but I wasn't saved out of drugs or wild living. Nor was I delivered from a satanic cult or a hardcore 80s rock band with subliminal messages. I'm like many Christians who've gone to church all their lives and have always done what they were told to do. So there it is – back to boring….

…But there is a generation of us out there. Sometimes we can think we don't have a testimony because we haven't stepped out of the lines and wrongly believe no one wants to listen to someone who's never really lived.

I also see plenty of young Christian people on the edge of adulthood looking at what the world offers. Yes, it's enticing to stick one pinky toe over to the other side. To dabble in the grey! I mean, you can always come back, right? God's grace is never-ending. Yes, it is, but from a girl whose life is seemingly extremely ordinary, I'm here to tell you, I've found something brilliantly extraordinary in chasing God with all my heart every day of my life. And it's NOT BORING! It's incredible and beautiful. It's joyful and fun and it's actually pretty great. But sometimes, I fall into the trap of thinking it's not, and that's when I need a good slap! Yet God never slaps me. He just patiently leads me back. He leads me back to remembering that it's cool to be BORING!

Chapter 1

My Story

The Normal, not so Norm of it All

So, how did it all begin for me? Well, I was just a kid, living in the suburbs, doing what kids used to do in suburban Brisbane way back in the late 70s, early 80s. Even back then, everything was pretty much run of the mill. My Dad had an accounting business, and my Mum was at home with my older sister and me. We had two dogs, a black Labrador named Dora (FYI, this was way before Dora the Explorer) and a Cavalier King Charles Spaniel, named Penelope and, that was that. But everything wasn't quite all that. My Mum was sick. She'd been ill all her life and pretty much didn't have a great life expectancy.

Somehow despite this, my memory of childhood is a happy one. I don't really remember my Mum being sick and lying around in bed feeling sorry for herself. However, I do remember her always being there for me and that we seemed to be constantly having fun adventures as a family. Obviously, I could only see things through a young child's worldview because things weren't that great. My Mum was very ill, and both Mum and Dad were getting desperate for things to change.

Oh, but let me take a step back because I'm getting ahead of myself. It all started with me. You see, I was sick too. Nothing major debilitating, but it wasn't that great either. I had reflux kidneys, and there wasn't much known about this disease or how to treat it. Fortunately for me, I was under the care of a doctor who, at the time, was one of the leading experts in his field. His name was Doctor Hurst. Poor guy, I wasn't a fan of him because every time I saw him, he seemed to inflict pain upon me, which earned him the nickname, Dr. Hurt Me (I know it's mean, but hey, I was only one and a half at the time).

Anyway, one day at home, I stopped breathing, and my Mum panicked, which is understandable. My Nana was there at the time (she often was because of Mum being sick), and she gave me mouth-to-mouth resuscitation and brought me back to life. While that was going on, my Mum had run outside to see if she could get help. We were one of the only houses in a new area, named Carindale, and there were a few workers around, and that was it. My Mum cried out for help, and when no one responded, she cried out again, this time to God asking Him to save her baby. Then she made a deal with Him. If He gave her my life back, she would spend the rest of her days working for Him, paying Him back, so to speak, for giving her my life.

Bargaining for Salvation

And so began our journey towards finding God. I went on to have surgery when I was about two years old to reverse this condition. After that, my parents began their journey in trying to pay God back for restoring my life. We started attending church and were pretty religious about it. We went regularly, put money in the offering plate, and volunteered at every event and working bee. Still, all the while, we never knew God. And my Mum, well, she was getting sicker and sicker.

My Mum had a disease called Bronchiectasis. It is a condition in which the lungs' airways widen due to chronic inflammation and infection. It results in irreversible damage to the lungs, characterised by re-current chest infections. My Mum was one of the more severe cases. She coughed up blood every day, struggled to walk upstairs and could do very little physical activity. Because the damage to her lungs was so significant, when she was 17, she had to have most of her left lung removed. Like many surgeries, there were risks and implications. To remove the lung, she had to have a rib removed. She also lost feeling on the left side of her back because the nerve endings were severed. The removal of her lung resulted in a space in her chest cavity. To compensate for this, her right lung and heart became enlarged to fill up this space. After the surgery, her right lung and what was left of her left lung kept collapsing. As a result, she had a subsequent procedure called a talc pleurodesis, which resulted in her having chronic pleurisy. All in all, this life my Mum was living was falling short of all that it could be.

And Then, there was a God Moment

One day my Mum was in the hospital, and a woman told her about a man on TV named Fred Price, who spoke about a God who heals. My Mum had never heard such a thing before. Can God heal people? She told my Dad about this, and they began trying to find out everything they could about God healing people. They watched Pastor Fred Price on TV, and they started reading the Bible to find out if it was true. Can God heal?

In February 1984, Fred Price came to Brisbane, Australia. It was the last time he ever came to Australia. He was here for a week, and my Dad took the entire week off work, which was unheard of, but things were desperate. My Mum had tried everything, and there was nothing left to do, so maybe this God thing could be the answer they were looking for.

The Day I Gave My Whole Heart to Jesus

The Sunday before the crusade began, there was a meeting at the Springwood Hotel. My sister and I attended a kid's meeting while my parents were in the main church. At the end of the session, there was a call for salvation. My sister leant over to me and told me I needed to put my hand up. I asked her if she would put her hand up as well, and she said to me she had already given her life to Jesus. Seeing as she was my big sister, I figured she knew what she was talking about, so I put up my hand. I went to another room with all the other kids who had put up their hands, where we prayed, and I asked Jesus into my heart. That was the day I said yes to Jesus. The day I gave Him my whole heart, and to this day, He has completely and truly had my whole heart. I've never taken it back. I am His forever!

After we prayed and asked Jesus into our hearts, the people running the kids' program invited us to receive the Holy Spirit and speak in other tongues. I was like, "Cool, I'll be able to speak in another language!" So they prayed, and just like they said, I spoke in tongues. It was that simple, childlike. Then I went back to where all the other kids were. The children's workers explained to the rest of the group that after we gave our lives to Jesus, we were filled with the Holy Spirit and could speak in other languages. They then asked if any of the other kids would like prayer for this. Now it was my turn to tell my sister that she should do this. So off she went, and she was filled with the Holy Spirit too!

Excitedly at the end of the meeting, we rushed to our parents and told them I was saved and that we could both speak in tongues. At first, they freaked out about our announcement, but they didn't rebuke us. Instead, they asked us questions and decided to look into what the

Bible said about it and see if there was any age limit to speaking in tongues. To their surprise, there wasn't. And so, even though my Mum and Dad weren't saved yet, they encouraged us to keep praying in this new language that God had given us. My parents were so soft and open to God at this time, and I am grateful that they embraced what God was doing in our lives and didn't try to quench our hunger by querying anything.

Healed...

All week long, my parents attended these meetings. By Friday night, God had them primed, and both my parents gave their lives to God that night. My Mum went down for healing, and she said she knew God was going to heal her. From the time that she heard about Fred Price until this event, it was about six months. In this time, my mother had read and reread practically every scripture there was to read about healing. A favourite of hers is from Mark 5:25-34. This is the story about the woman with the issue of blood. My Mum held on in faith, believing that, like this woman, she just had to reach out and touch Jesus, and she would be healed. And that's precisely what she did.

As Pastor Fred Price was coming down the line laying hands on people, God touched my Mother. Two people before Pastor Fred Price touched my Mum, she was slain in the spirit. She went down a sick woman with very little hope and came up saved and healed! Immediately she could feel freedom in her airways. She could breathe like never before. She stopped coughing up blood and could walk upstairs without feeling breathless. She stopped taking her medication and has never looked back. It was a miracle!

As a family, we were radically saved, and from that time on, we began chasing God with enthusiasm and passion. My parents started Bible college almost immediately. We became planted in a Pentecostal church that saw us growing in God's ways. Everything was good. However, I've learnt God doesn't just settle with good. In ***John 10:10 (TPT)*** it says,

> *I have come to give you everything in abundance, more than you expect – life in its fullness until you overflow!*

And that's what He was about to do for my family.

...And Whole

Fast forward to October 1984, and a guest speaker was at our church. At the end of the service, he asked people to stand up and place their hands on the part of their body that needed healing. My Mum stood up and put her hand on her heart. She asked God to continue the work He had begun in her and heal anything that still needed healing. That afternoon as my parents were getting ready for church, my Dad tickled my Mum's side. She said, "Do that again. I felt you touch me." Remember I mentioned when my Mum had surgery at 17 to remove her lung, all her nerve endings were severed? Since that time, she had no feeling on her left side…

…Until now.

When my Dad touched her the second time, he noticed something. There was no gap in her side where the rib had been removed. He counted down the left side of her back, and all her ribs were there! The next day my Mum went and had a chest X-ray, and the results showed a perfectly normal chest. Two perfectly healthy lungs, a normal-sized heart, and all her ribs. God hadn't only healed my Mum. Like the woman with the issue of blood, He had made her whole, and in the process, He had made our entire family whole.

Something Special was Happening in Me

While all this was happening, something else was happening that we didn't notice straight away. Healing also came to me. Sometime during all that God was doing in my Mum's life and my family, the problems and side effects from reflux kidneys went away. God is so good! The doctors told my parents that due to the severity of the disease, I would most likely have side effects throughout my life, and they could stunt my growth. Well, I'm not a six-foot giant or anything, but I am just under 175cm tall, which is not short by any means for a woman. I've also had no other symptoms or side effects since I gave my life to Jesus at six years. So in my heart, I honestly believe not only did God give my Mum a new lung and rib, but He also gave me new kidneys.

> ***Ephesians 3:20 (TPT)*** *says,*
>
> *Never doubt God's mighty power to work in you and accomplish all this. He will achieve infinitely more than your greatest request, your most unbelievable dream and exceed your wildest imagination! He will out do them all, for His miraculous power constantly energises you.*

He certainly did this for me! I love that God is no respecter of persons. He saved my entire family, and He met each of our individual needs.

There is Power in Your Story Too!

Okay, so that is quite some testimony! On the scale of phenomenal salvation stories, it goes off the charts! Yes, I have to admit, I was radically saved. I'm not ashamed of it because this is my story - my testimony. It's how my Psalm 1 journey began.

You may be reading this and thinking, "Wow, my testimony of finding God can't compare to that!" Well, it shouldn't have to. Every Christian walk begins with giving your life to Jesus. The how of this process is equally beautiful and spectacular for every individual. The Bible tells us that God chases after the one, and when He finds the one, there is an exuberant celebration in Heaven. No more or less because the how was more impressive for some than it was for others.

My sister gave her heart to Jesus in her bed. Then she got out of bed and knelt beside it and prayed again in case she hadn't done it quite right the first time. I gave my life to Jesus in a kids' meeting, and my Mum, well, she was miraculously healed. For everyone, it will be different. My husband has a unique story, and so do each of my children. What is paramount is that you have a story, and you know that it is unique to you and that God lovingly chose that specific moment in time to bring you to Him.

Psalm 1:1 (TPT) *says,*

What delight comes to the one who follows God's ways!

Start Your Journey Today

Our journey following Christ begins by choosing to follow Him, and then from there, we walk out this journey every day. The first step is to choose to follow Him. If you have never done that before, the Bible teaches that all you need to do for salvation is to confess with your mouth and believe in your heart that Jesus is Lord. You don't have to earn God's love and salvation, and you don't have to wait to be perfect before you give your life to Him. You can do it right now, and if it's something you've never done before, I encourage you to do so now by saying this simple prayer:

Heavenly Father, thank you for sending Your son Jesus to die for me. Thank you for raising Him from the dead so that I might be free. I know I can't do anything to earn this gift of love. You have done it all. I ask you to forgive me of my sins. I confess you are Lord of my life and believe in You with my whole heart. From this day forward, I will follow You. In Jesus mighty and precious name. Amen!

That's it. You are saved, and all of Heaven is joining in the celebration! This is now your story of coming to Christ, and it is an especially beautiful one!

Remember Your Story and Share It with Others

For those who are already saved, this is an excellent opportunity to reflect on that beautiful moment - the moment when you began your journey of walking with Him. Take time now to remember your time of salvation and what led you to that moment. Praise Him for His gift of salvation and all that He has done for you since that time. Then, sit down with your family and remember how each one of you came to give your lives to Jesus. There is so much power in that, and I think it's crucial for our kids, grandkids and other family members to know these stories. It is such a fundamental part of our heritage and legacy. We don't reflect on this time in our lives enough. It was a momentous occasion, and we should never downplay it. Every single one of us has a testimony, and we can use that testimony to:

1. Build ourselves up by remembering that precious moment in our lives
2. Encourage and uplift others by sharing what God has done for us
3. Tell others about God's love and plan for salvation for their lives

Remember this, your moment of salvation and testimony is your unique story. I believe no two testimonies are the same. Your testimony is also a mighty sword in your hand that can affect change in you and those around you. Never be ashamed to proclaim it from the mountaintops. I have heard my mother's salvation story hundreds, maybe thousands of times, and I have told my salvation story on as many occasions. I've never tired of hearing it or telling it, and I'm yet to meet a person who didn't want to listen. So let's rise up and make a conscious decision that in our day-to-day seemingly mundane lives, we will be more proactive about sharing our salvation stories. Watch what a difference it will make to your life and the lives of those with whom you share your story.

Chapter 2

Fog

One of the most beautiful things about giving your life to Jesus is that the moment of conversion is just the beginning. Christianity is not a moment in time. It is a faith walk, a journey. Each day we walk out our decision to follow Christ, and each day is an opportunity to experience the wonder of His grace. Typically, in the beginning, everything is new and exciting and promising, but eventually, at some point, the concerns of life will test our faith. Learning to trust in and rely on God daily can be one of the toughest challenges for Christians, whether newly saved or saved for many, many years. So how do we do that? How do we stop worrying about the concerns that creep into our lives? Jesus talks about this very thing in ***Matthew 6:25-34 (NIV)***. This is what he says:

> *Therefore I tell you, do not worry about your life, what you will eat or drink; or about your body, what you will wear. Is not life more than food, and the body more than clothes? Look at the birds*

of the air; they do not sow or reap or store away in barns, and yet your Heavenly Father feeds them. Are you not much more valuable than they? Can any one of you by worrying add a single hour to your life? And why do you worry about clothes? See how the flowers of the field grow. They do not labor or spin. Yet I tell you that not even Solomon in all his splendor was dressed like one of these. If that is how God clothes the grass of the field, which is here today and tomorrow is thrown into the fire, will he not much more clothe you — you of little faith? So do not worry, saying, "What shall we eat?" or "What shall we drink?" or "What shall we wear?" For the pagans run after all these things, and your Heavenly Father knows that you need them. But seek first his kingdom and his righteousness, and all these things will be given to you as well. Therefore do not worry about tomorrow, for tomorrow will worry about itself. Each day has enough trouble of its own.

Worry. In many ways, worry seems to rule the world these days. There is probably not a day that goes by that we don't worry about something. On a scale of one to ten, worries can be all that and more: little worries, medium worries, big worries. Worry is a genuine thing. Nothing is new under the sun, though. That is why Jesus specifically addressed it during His time on earth. By the sound of things, even back then, the Israelites were prolific worriers. Jesus knew things wouldn't change thousands of years later. His message then still rings true today. Don't worry. Easier said than done, right? So how do we not worry? Jesus told his disciples that the key was to seek His kingdom first. What does this mean, and how do we do this? Well, I believe nature's fog phenomena can shed some light on this and perhaps a lot more...

There is Always Purpose in the Fog

A few years ago, I travelled with my family on holiday to America. Eleven of us travelled altogether, including my clan, my Mum and Dad, and my sister and her family. What a hoot we had!! We visited so many incredible places and had bucket loads of fun in the process. It will be a holiday we will all remember for the rest of our lives.

One of the places we visited was San Fransisco. San Fransisco is a charming place, and we loved our time there. Above everything else, one thing struck me as quite astonishing: the fog, thick, heavy, misty fog. San Fransisco is famous for fog. It seems to roll in early in the morning and can hang around until the middle of the day. The San Fransisco Fog is not just famous. It's infamous. So much so, that it is lovingly named 'Karl the Fog.' It even has its own Instagram page!

While I was in San Fransisco and for a long time after that, I was fascinated and intrigued by 'Karl the Fog'. Initially, I thought how annoying it would be to live in a place that was always foggy because fog limits visibility, but then a scripture came to mind:

Genesis 1:1-4 (The Voice)

In the beginning, God created everything: the Heavens above and the earth below. Here's what happened: At first the earth lacked shape and was totally empty, and a dark fog draped over the deep while God's spirit-wind hovered over the surface of the empty waters. Then there was the voice of God. "Let there be light." And light flashed into being. God saw that the light was beautiful and good, and He separated the light from the darkness.

I realised just because there may not be clarity doesn't mean God isn't there (hovering getting ready to speak over your life). Right from the very beginning, when there seemed to be nothing but a shapeless, empty place covered with fog, God was there. Likewise, there can be times in life when nothing makes sense. And I mean nothing, but God is always there.

One thing that comes to my mind is when nothing seems to be going my way, even though I have done everything right. Have you ever had one of those conversations with God that kind of goes like this, "God, it's so unfair! I've always done the right thing. I never do anything wrong. I've been faithful to you all my life. So I don't understand. Why aren't things working out for me?"

One of the most fascinating things about fog is it lifts, but it does so ever so slowly, and as it does, it gradually reveals the scenery hiding behind it. We see this reflected in the story of creation. When God spoke, light broke through the fog, and it was beautiful and good. The fog may have seemed to have no purpose. However, God was present in the mist, and it was through the fog He spoke and brought forth form and meaning to the earth. The Bible promises God will never leave us or forsake us. What God says is true, and if He says He will never leave us, then we can rest in the knowledge that even through the fog, He is always there.

There are Always Opportunities for Discovery Amidst the Fog

One day stands out in my memory during our time in San Francisco – the day we walked to see the Golden Gate Bridge (which was a great deal further than we had anticipated and made for quite the journey with several kids in tow). It was a day much like I described above. It started with heavy fog, bleak, dreary, and cold. No one was that excited about walking through fog, and we were all doubtful as to whether we would even get to see the bridge. So, we were all trudging along. As we went along, we began to notice beautiful things even amongst the fog. The way the fog settled over the bay and the fishing trawlers. The way it hugged the shore and made it seem like we were in a sleepy coastal village from ages past.

Life can be a lot like that. It can feel like the fog is all around us, and we can feel uncertain of where we're heading, but when your vision is limited, where will you choose to direct your focus? Are you going to focus on the fog, or are you prepared to enjoy the marvellous things right before your eyes? No, they may not be the end result, but that doesn't mean those small things can't bring you joy, and you can't enjoy the journey or the process.

Let's consider the Fruits of the Spirit. I think they are ordered this way for a reason. Love is first, and we all know love is first and foremost, but it's closely followed by joy. Why is that? I believe it's because joy is a product of love. The revelation of God's unconditional love for us enables us to love this way too, and as we walk out in love, joy can't help but flow from our lives.

Secondly, I believe God wants us to find joy in all things. Not just when we arrive, but every step of the way. I have the most wonderful husband, he's handsome and clever, he's caring and creative and good with his hands. He's approachable and the sort of guy you can't help but like, and he makes everyone feel accepted and comfortable. So many admirable qualities, but he is also hilariously funny and quick-witted, and he makes me laugh. Even in the most serious and sombre moments, he can say something to make me laugh. It's so good for me because I can be so intense at times, but my husband always seems to know how to help me stop and find joy in the most mundane of things. The day we walked to see the Golden Gate Bridge was no different. I can distinctively remember my husband saying things to make everyone laugh, which completely lightened the mood.

Get Ready for the Big Reveal

Gradually as we walked and talked and began noticing these things, our moods changed even though the fog around us hadn't. Then suddenly, the fog started lifting, and the warm rays of the sun began to shine through. There was a new energy in our steps as warmth filled us. And then we began to see it. Only glimpses at first, but it was there. In fact, it had been there all along, and as the fog drifted away, one of the most beautiful sights I've ever seen was right before my eyes. The Golden Gate Bridge in all its glory! And oh my, it was glorious! Just like that, all the dreariness and tiredness (and hunger by that stage) vanished. What we had been journeying towards was right there. I laugh now as I think about how the Golden Gate Bridge was there all along, but the fog was so thick and heavy that we literally couldn't see it at all.

God spoke to me at that moment, asking, "Are you prepared to wait for Me to speak My words over your situation, gradually revealing My master plan for your life as I see fit? Can you trust in what you can't see? Are you willing to step out in faith and walk towards something you can't see? Can you trust that when the fog lifts, it's going to be magnificent?" It's exciting when you think about it.

The first time I met my husband, I was 15, and he was 16. We met at an inter-school athletics carnival, and a mutual friend introduced us. I remember I wasn't very impressed when I met him, wondering what was so great about him? I know he didn't think much about me either at the time because he doesn't even remember meeting me! Both of us had limited visibility. We couldn't see through the fog. However, I'm confident God was sitting up in Heaven having a good ol' chuckle and saying to all of Heaven, "Those two down there, they don't think much of each other now, but little do they know, they're going to fall in love and get married one day!" It was about three years later that we met for the second time, and well, I guess you could say we made a much better impression on one another!

Keep Your Cool when the Fog Rolls In

Another distinctive characteristic about 'Karl the Fog' is it provides cooling to the coastal communities in summer when inland is experiencing tremendous heat. I love this! When the world is experiencing trouble, worry, anxiety and terror, we as Christians can keep our cool because the presence of God's fog is all around us. We might not be able to see the end plan, but we don't need to sweat it because the mist of God's presence brings peace.

Remember I said the Fruit of the Spirit was ordered in a particular way for a reason? Love first, which leads to joy. As we walk in joy, complete peace comes even amid challenges and trials. When we cultivate an attitude of love and joy, peace automatically follows. Let's take a moment to ponder on the peace that comes when God's fog of favour descends upon our lives.

Philippians 4:4-9 (NIV)

Rejoice in the Lord always. I will say it again: Rejoice! Let your gentleness be evident to all. The Lord is near. Do not be anxious about anything, but in every situation, by prayer and petition, with thanksgiving, present your requests to God. And the peace of God, which transcends all understanding, will guard your hearts and your minds in Christ Jesus. Finally, brothers and sisters, whatever is true, whatever is noble, whatever is right, whatever is pure, whatever is lovely, whatever is admirable – if anything is excellent or praiseworthy – think about such things. Whatever you have learned or received or heard from me, or seen in me – put it into practice. And the God of peace will be with you.

I love Philippians 4:4-9. It is probably my favourite scripture in the Bible. I know it by heart, and it is so special to me. When I was a child, I had some graphic nightmares that were detailed and vivid and are still very clear in my memory. As a child, they terrified me and bound me with fear. At night I had terrible problems falling asleep. So every night, my Dad would sit by my bed and read these verses repeatedly until I fell asleep. He did this for a long time. Eventually, I learnt to recite these verses myself over and over again. Often my Dad would check on me – I'd be asleep with my Bible open on my chest to this very passage. He would take the Bible, close it and slip it under my pillow. I recited these verses and slept with a Bible under my pillow every night until the day I was married.

I continue to love these verses in my adult life and have learned they have many applications for living as a Christian beyond a good, peaceful night's rest. Verses 8 and 9 provide a powerful list of standards we should live by. They outline what we should look at, think about, and speak about and how our actions should reflect Christ. I don't think God's word can be any clearer. In fact, He's making it easy for us to know how we should be living. So if you have a moral dilemma or find yourself in a compromising situation, if you can't find your way through all the grey to know what to do, Paul's words in Philippians can bring clarity:

Whatever is true, whatever is noble...

I use these words to help me in small areas, like should I watch this TV program or listen to this song, or be gossiping about my friend, or post this on insta? To the really big things e.g. when anxiety rages, when the world is under threat of virus, wars, terror – when I am faced with sickness, financial pressures, difficult relationships. When my mind is focusing on the negative, I come back to this verse, and I say it over and over until I can sense the peace of God settling like a fog over my heart.

But the next verse is equally impressive and perhaps even more powerful because it's a call to action, and it sets the bar for our standard of living even higher. That's not to say we have to strive or work for it. Instead, we live it out through undeserved grace and love that God has lavished upon us.

Verse 9 says,

Whatever you have learned or received or heard from me, or seen in me – put it into practice. And the God of peace will be with you.

Wow! The key to peace is following in Jesus' footsteps. Doing what we have learned and received and heard and seen Him do. As we walk the journey of life, walking towards the ultimate prize of eternal fellowship with our Father in Heaven, we walk in the fog of His presence. His presence brings peace that passes all understanding, and we do this by living like Him.

When the Fog Embodies

Who would have thought you could learn so much from fog? Well, I'm not done yet. This is probably my favourite thing about fog because it also combines one of my other loves, trees. When it comes to trees, I'm a bit obsessed, so I'll devote a chapter to trees a little later.

While visiting San Fransisco, we took a day trip to see the Redwood Trees in Muir Woods. If you love trees, this place should be on your bucket list. I've never seen such mind-blowing trees with gigantic trunks you can't even wrap your arms around that stretch to the Heavens. It's such a sight to behold. The forest is all the more mystical because of the lingering fog that seems to hover around it and follow you wherever you go.

Even after we left the forest that day, I couldn't help but think about those trees and how glorious they were. I also wondered about 'Karl the Fog' and whether there was any significance between the fog and the trees. So I began to do a little bit of research and discovered some surprising things about fog and the Redwood Forests.

I discovered fog is crucial to the well-being of Redwood Forests, playing a necessary part in their life cycle. The Redwood tree has many characteristics that allows it to intercept the fog as it passes through the forest. Water droplets in fog precipitate onto the needles of the tree, and some are absorbed. The rest drops to the ground, which provides an essential source of moisture in the Redwood Forest.

One article I read said, "In one foggy night, a single Redwood can douse the ground beneath it with the equivalent of a drenching rainstorm."[1] The author went on to say, "I've never been more wet in my life than I have been in the Redwood Forest during a major fog event. You're soaking wet when you're underneath one."[2]

As I reflected on these things, it was undeniable that this was an example of creation mirroring the heart of God. In this case, fog represents the presence of God or the Holy Spirit and the Redwoods, His people – us. The other species in the forest represent those around us who are yet to know Christ. We can learn from this life parable that we need to possess the characteristics to be good at intercepting spiritual fog. As we receive the Holy Spirit fog, He will soak and drench us with His presence. The exciting part is, it will not only benefit us, but it will also impact those around us. In a world where there doesn't seem

---

[1] Carol Kaesong Yoon, "Clues to Redwoods' Mighty Growth Emerge in Fog," *New York Times,* Nov. 24, 1998.
[2] Ibid.

to be enough water and nourishment for humans to grow, God's fog is descending upon spiritual Redwood forests so that tree, upon tree, upon tree can be generously nourished and watered and can grow to astounding, phenomenal heights.

Interestingly, fog means survival for many Bay Area plants and animals. It is crucial to both the Redwoods' survival but also the survival of many species. Deforestation implies the fog can't be absorbed, which is detrimental to the Redwoods and other plant and animal life in the forests.

The devil wants to cut down spiritual trees however he can to achieve spiritual deforestation. He uses many sneaky tactics to take out whoever he can – young and old. He will spare no generation.

So how can we stop this? Well, we need to be intercepting and being doused in spiritual fog regularly. Just like fog, God's presence is crucial to our well-being and growth. We can't have an impact on others until we first nourish ourselves with everything of Him. How do I do this, you may be asking? Well, simply put, spend time with Him. His presence is ushered by reading His Word, spending time in prayer, praise and worship and being in His house. All these things draw us nearer to Him and surround us with His presence.

The beauty of God's presence is that it is for more than just you. Once you have received the gift of His presence, it can't help but overflow and touch others. That is the way God operates – He uses people to spread His presence. Take out the people, and God's presence can't have an impact. That means God needs you and me to be spiritual Redwoods that will intercept His beautiful peace and presence, allowing it to flow through us and spread to the spiritual forest around us. So don't shy away from or underestimate the power of God's presence. It is detrimental not only to our survival but also to the survival of those around us.

One of the most powerful ways we can embody the fog of God's presence is through worship. Worship holds a very special place in my heart, so I think it is deserving of its own chapter – or maybe two.

Chapter 3

The Better Thing

Do you ever think about Heaven?
    What will it look like?
    Who will be there?
    What might you do there?
    It's not like I think about it all the time, but I do think about it and try to imagine what it might be like.
    Sometimes I imagine the moment when I finally get there and see my Father God face to face. Other times I think of crazy things. For example, my favourite thing to eat is strawberries. In my opinion, they are the most divine fruit. I love them so much that my wedding cake consisted of tiers of strawberry tarts with one big strawberry tart in the shape of a heart on top! Anyway, sometimes I imagine what strawberries will be like in Heaven. I imagine they are so big and juicy and when I taste them, they will be the most scrumptious, divine thing I've ever

tasted. Crazy hey? But I believe God wants us to imagine Heaven and all the different aspects of it, even if it's not very theologically sound.

Another thing I think about is who I will meet when I get there. Have you ever thought about that? Or asked yourself, "After I meet Father God and Jesus, who is the first person I want to meet in Heaven?" Maybe you've never thought about it. I have, and while there are many people I want to meet like, David, Joseph, Ruth, Esther, Abraham and Sarah, Peter, Paul, Darlene Zschech and I could go on, there's one person who tops the list. She's a woman, of course, and I would love to sit down with her and sip on delectable Heavenly coffee and have a really good chat. So, who would this person be, you ask? Well, my number one person that I want to meet when I get to Heaven is Mary, Mary Magdalene.

I have always loved the story of Mary anointing Jesus's feet at Bethany. Over the many years that I have been a Christian, it's one of the stories in the Bible I go back to time and time again. There always seems to be something new that the Holy Spirit shows me concerning worship and my relationship with God. However, to best understand the significance of this story, we need to first look at the passage about Mary and Martha in **Luke 10:38-42 (TPT)**.

As Jesus and the disciples continued on their journey, they came to a village where a woman welcomed Jesus into her home. Her name was Martha and she had a sister named Mary. Mary sat down attentively before the Master, absorbing every revelation he shared. But Martha became exasperated by finishing the numerous household chores in preparation for her guests, so she interrupted Jesus and said, "Lord, don't you think it's unfair that my sister left me to do all the work by myself? You should tell her to get up and help me."

The Lord answered her, "Martha, my beloved Martha. Why are you upset and troubled, pulled away by all these many distractions? Are they really that important? Mary has discovered the one thing most important by choosing to sit at my feet. She is undistracted, and I won't take this privilege from her."

There's No Place for Perfectionism in the Presence of Grace

For some reason, I always feel a bit sorry for Martha in this story. She was trying so hard to impress Jesus, but she had missed the one thing Jesus wanted. If I'm honest, I have often approached God with a similar attitude to Martha. I think if we are honest with ourselves, we could all say the same. But you see, the point of this story is all about works versus grace.

I've been saved for over thirty years. I've heard the message of grace preached eons of times. I believe I know and understand God's grace in both my head and heart, but I don't always walk it out. Living in a performance-focused society, I can slip into a Martha mindset more often than I'm proud to admit. Martha was wearing herself out trying to impress Jesus with what SHE could do and with HER skills. She became increasingly frustrated because SHE was doing all this incredible stuff – stuff that typically would impress any other human being. Yet, Jesus wasn't moved by her abilities and performance whatsoever. OUCH!!

When I compare myself to Mary and Martha, I would love to say I'm totally all Mary, but if I'm being real and honest, which is what I am trying to be in this book, I'm probably more like Martha. It may come as a surprise to some, but I have flaws (I know shock horror)! One of my most significant flaws is I am a Perfectionist, and I get the feeling, Martha was one too. Perfectionism has been my undoing one too many times. There is a fine line between excellence and perfectionism, and when you cross that line, no matter how brilliant, or outstanding something you've done might be, there's no turning back. When you're a perfectionist, all you see are the flaws, usually minuscule and of little significance to anyone else. The problem is it can suck the joy out of something that should have been wonderful and really great. Suddenly you become a 'Perfect-Zilla', and you're always grumpy. Firstly at yourself for not being perfect (even though you know it's completely unrealistic) and then at everything and everyone around you cos nothing, especially you, is ever good enough.

Case in point: One time (okay, cos my Mum is reading this maybe on numerous occasions), I may have had a meltdown because I felt I hadn't done as well on an assignment at Uni as I would have liked. Anyway, this one particular time, I had worked extremely hard and had juggled a whole bunch of stuff like running a family and a business amongst the COVID-19 pandemic. I felt I had done a great job on the paper I wrote, and when I got my result back, it wasn't what I had expected. I was devastated and perhaps, maybe, quite possibly… hysterical. I pretty much gave up all hope of doing well in the subject, even though I knew all my other assessments results were near-perfect grades. It turned out that miraculously I scraped through and received a High Distinction! However, when I got the result, I wasn't excited about it. I convinced myself I didn't deserve it because one of my assignments wasn't up to my excellent standard. My desire to be perfect had robbed me of the joy I should have experienced for doing a great job and receiving the highest grade at a University level course.

I could almost hear Jesus whispering to me:

"Andrina, my beloved Andrina. Why are you upset and troubled, pulled away by all these many distractions? Are they really that important?"

In the spirit of being truthful, I have also, on many occasions, been like how I imagine Martha would have been that day. You know, busy around the house doing all the things that needed doing. Silently hoping someone in my family would notice, and by some miracle, offer to lend a hand without any prompting. Which, of course, doesn't happen, so then I have to do the work with extra effort, subtly or not so subtly banging things, sighing, and moaning so my family will notice and join in to help. But to no avail!

I keep working as my patience diminishes and my frustration increases, until I can't hold it in any longer and like Martha blurt out something like, "Do I have to do everything around here? Doesn't anyone care that I'm doing all the work?" And then a whole bunch of ranting and raving follows about how nobody helps, and when they do, it's always half-hearted, and I have to come behind and fix everything resulting in more work for me. Insert eye roll here!! Of course, I know all this upsets everyone and makes them less inclined to want to help. Yet, in the spirit of perfectionism, I still do it. I just never seem to learn.

That was pretty much Martha the day Jesus came to her house – working hard, doing everything in her own strength. Trying so hard to impress Him with her perfection, but all it was doing was making her miserable.

One of the biggest pitfalls of perfectionism is it can be tough to accept grace because perfectionism is addictive. For me, there is nothing more satisfying than doing something perfectly and getting rewarded for it. Every time I do something phenomenal, I get a high from what I've achieved. It's not necessarily about impressing others with what I can do and earning praise from people. As a true perfectionist, the satisfaction is in knowing my efforts got me to this place of success.

It is dangerously addictive, and there is no place for grace when this mindset rules. The struggle for perfectionists is if they receive grace, they don't have to strive, which goes against their very makeup. Perfectionism is all about striving and getting it right 100% of the time. It is a massive shift for a perfectionist (for want of a better phrase) *'to let go and let God'*, and one that Martha was clearly struggling to grasp.

There is Something so Beautiful when we Exchange Perfectionism for His Presence

Mary, on the other hand, had discovered a compelling truth. Nothing she could do would ever be enough. WOW! Now, typically coming to that conclusion about yourself would be very hurtful, but for Mary it wasn't, because Mary was beginning to learn the true meaning of grace – you can't earn it. So realising this, Mary decided to sit in the presence of Jesus and soak in everything of Him that she could.

This is a tremendous key. Being still before God, sitting in His presence, waiting upon Him. God wants to pour His love, His grace, His revelation into us. He wants us to receive before we give. He wants us to spend time with Him, reclining in his love. Just like it says in **Psalm 46:10a (NIV):**

Be still and know that I am God.

The Passion Translation says it so aptly:

Surrender your anxiety!
Be silent and stop your striving and you will see that I am God.

God wants us to be deliberate about being still because when we are still, He can show us more of who He is. Sometimes we are so busy living out our lives we can forget who God is. The day Mary sat at Jesus' feet, she had a revelation about her Saviour. The beautiful, extravagant act of worship she is known for followed the act of sitting at his feet. Sometimes in our worship, we are so focused on how we are worshipping, and we overlook the moments of stillness where God wants to pour into us.

I liken it to my relationship with my husband or my children. Sometimes it's just lovely to hug and cuddle them. We might not say anything, but we know that we are loved by being held. If that is how I am with the people I love here on earth, and being made in the image of God, then how much more does God want to do that to me. He desires to embrace me, be with me, pour into me. That isn't going to happen if I'm always doing and always trying to be perfect. I need to be still, just as I am. If I wait until I am perfect or what I think is ideal in my own eyes, I will never be ready or enough for God's presence.

So Choose the Better Thing

That is why Mary chose the better thing that day. She stopped trying to be perfect and let go of the doing, the impressing and the earning. Instead, she made herself still and put herself in God's presence just as she was. In the place of stillness and being with Jesus, Mary was able to receive the fullness of His love and the revelation that without first obtaining the fullness of Christ's love, we are nothing.

Jesus was inviting Martha to do the same. He could see her desire to be perfect would only lead to her being exhausted, burnt out, and bitter, and He knew that wasn't good for her. So he showed her a way she could live the abundant life, as it says in ***Matthew 11:28 (NIV):***

Come to me all who are weary and burdened and I will give you rest.

So how do I deal with perfectionism? Well, I recognise it's a part of the way I'm wired, and because I am very goal-driven and want to achieve, it's not something that will go away. However, when it consumes me, I need to be able to let it go. I need to release it to my Saviour, Jesus, and sit with Him.

There is a place I like to sit in the morning in my lounge room that looks out over our property and all the beautiful trees we have. Most mornings, I sit there as I drink my coffee, and I talk to God. My family is usually all buzzing around me, but silently, without them knowing, I have my daily hug with God. I typically say something like, "Here I am God, I'm ready for my hug," and for a brief moment or two, I am held, held by my Father God, the Maker of Heaven and earth. And that's what keeps me grounded because when my God holds me, nothing else matters but Him and me. Although I can't see Him or feel His physical arms around me, it is one of the most honest moments in my day, and I know He is there with me, barely a breath away. It's the time of the day when it's not about me. I'm not perfectly groomed or have everything together. I come to God as I am in that moment.

Today, right now, why don't you take a moment to be still in God's presence and be held by Him. Let go of all the things that are making you uptight, stressed, flustered, and worn out. Put them aside and be with God. Maybe you can pray this prayer:

"Father, I come before You today, to be with You. I put aside all the things I've been trying to do in my own strength to impress others and also to impress You. I know I don't need to do that, Your love is all I need. So today, I come with only one agenda – to sit with you. In Jesus name. Amen."

Chapter 4

The Beautiful Exchange

Have you ever given someone a present you were really excited to give to them? You know, the type of gift you've given a great deal of thought and planning to present to them? The very thing you knew was so perfect for that person. And then, you have to keep it a secret so it will be a surprise, but you can hardly contain yourself because you are bursting with excitement to see their face when they open the gift. Then the moment finally comes to give them the present, and it turns out to be everything you hoped for and more. They love the gift and are completely ecstatic.

I remember one time, many years ago, my husband and sister planned a surprise trip to Melbourne for my birthday. They were acting all weird and secretive, so I was a bit suspicious that something was up. I remember when I found out I was going to Melbourne, how surprised and excited I was. But I also remember they were equally, if not more excited than I was. It was such an extraordinary gift, and we had the best weekend exploring Melbourne. We often reminisce about that birthday and the fun we had.

I like to tell the story of how my husband was trying so hard to be secretive and give me this fantastic gift. How he packed my bag for a weekend in Melbourne during May (which is late Autumn in Australia) and he didn't pack any warm clothes for me! Okay, one long sleeve shirt and a light cardigan, perfect for Autumn in Brisbane, but not Melbourne. Haha, it happened to be absolutely freezing that weekend. But, not to worry, it was the perfect excuse to shop (I actually bought the most beautiful coat, which I still wear today)! Despite my husband not getting it perfect, it never lessened the wonder of the gift. Hey, I'm still talking about it 17 years on!

Extravagant Yet Imperfect

I liken that experience to the time Mary anointed Jesus at Bethany. Have you ever stopped to think that maybe the Alabaster Box wasn't as perfect as we all think it was? Perhaps that's because it has a lot to do with Jesus and how He received the gift. I guess human nature causes us to worry about always having it perfect, even when we come to God. But as you'll see in this story, it is not about perfection at all. Let's take a look at the account given in ***John 12:1-8 (TPT)***

> *Six days before the Passover began, Jesus went back to Bethany, the town where he raised Lazarus from the dead. They had prepared a supper for Jesus. Martha served, and Lazarus and Mary were among those at the table. Mary picked up an alabaster jar filled with nearly a litre of extremely rare and costly perfume—the purest extract of nard, and she anointed Jesus' feet. Then she wiped them dry with her long hair. And the fragrance of the costly oil filled the house. But Judas the locksmith, Simon's son, the betrayer, spoke up and said,*

"What a waste! We could have sold this perfume for a fortune and given the money to the poor!" (In fact, Judas had no heart for the poor. He only said this because he was a thief and in charge of the money case. He would steal money whenever he wanted from the funds given to support Jesus' ministry.) Jesus said to Judas, "Leave her alone! She has saved it for the time of my burial. You'll always have the poor with you; but you won't always have me."

I have already mentioned I am a perfectionist, but I'm also very goal-driven. I like to always have something I'm working towards. It can be a work goal, a fitness goal, or even a relationship goal. It's always great to have a plan, but sometimes I can get wrapped up in the achievement. My vision gets clouded as I tell myself I'll be a better person if I achieve yet another goal. For some silly reason, I convince myself my family will be proud of me, and people will like and respect me more. The problem with that is it is never enough, and you find yourself constantly looking for the next conquest. In today's world, I feel like many share this mindset. We are all trying to prove ourselves to one another.

"Look at me and how 'awesome' I am!"

"Look at me and my 'awesome' children!"

"Look at me and my 'awesome' husband!"

"Aren't we the ultimate power couple!"

Can anyone relate?

We seem wired this way. Think about when you meet someone for the first time. On most occasions, one of the first questions we ask is, "What do you do?" If I do say so myself, my 'WHAT' list is pretty impressive for an ordinary girl:

Wife

Mother

Speech Pathologist

Business Owner

Masters Student
Church Volunteer
Wanna Be Author
And I could go on and give myself a nice little pat on the back.
Or…
…Before my head gets so big it explodes, let's take a look at the alabaster box.

The Value of the Alabaster Box

Each of the Gospels (Matthew 26:6-13, Mark 14:3-9, Luke 7:36-50, John 12:1-8) gives an account of a woman coming to anoint Jesus. There is much debate about whether these are the same woman, and quite likely they are not. However, it is not so much about who anointed Jesus, but rather the significance of the act.

Mary's gift was not given on a whim. It was a response to her sitting at Jesus' feet and soaking in His presence (remember the story in Luke 10:38-42). A response to a revelation – Mary was able to give because she had first received. That's why being in God's presence is so vital. We can't do or be anything without Him, and when we truly understand that, we will want nothing more than to run into the throne room of Heaven to be at His feet!

So to me, the alabaster box represents all the WHATs in our lives: the good, the bad and the ugly. Because for all the astonishing WHATs I've achieved, there is a truckload of WHATs I'd prefer not to share with anyone. However, when Mary sat at Jesus' feet, all the WHATs in the world meant nothing compared to WHO was in the room. When she came to anoint Jesus, she carried everything that she was in the alabaster box. All her titles, all her achievements, all her actions, all her mistakes, all her sins – EVERYTHING.

And then, she poured it all out.

The Beautiful Exchange

Because Mary had spent time sitting in Jesus' presence, she had complete trust that she could give everything without judgement or condemnation, and she would be completely safe. She knew her all could never measure up, but she also knew she had to give it all to be free from the bondage of life – from man's opinion of her, from all the WHATs that she could achieve. When she gave it all, Jesus showed her who she was, as a Daughter of the King. It's not what Mary poured out that was beautiful in this story – rather, it's the Beautiful Exchange. That is what makes beautiful, pure worship.

It's funny how in this passage, the people around were so indignant about how wasteful this act was. They were so caught up in WHAT the gift was – they missed the moment of truth. Jesus and Mary were sharing in a moment together. So much was being exchanged that I can't even put it into words. Yes, it was extravagant! It was extravagant because Mary gave her all. It was extravagant because she gave in response to God's presence. But more than this, it was extravagant because Jesus took all the alabaster box represented (her life in essence), and in return, He poured out so much love upon Mary.

Mary was able to do something in that moment that the Pharisees, the disciples, nor any other person had been able to do despite all their striving and law perfecting. She made it personal. At that time, she wholly and completely captured her Saviour's heart. She had Him because He had her.

I don't want to have to live my life always trying to measure up, trying to achieve, trying to be something I think people want me to be. I want to be authentic and genuine. Worship is the place where I am my truest self. I don't have to hide or pretend – I can be me. My Father knows all my faults. He knows I'm a work in progress. He knows my alabaster box isn't perfect, but He also knows its value, and when I bring it to Him, it is priceless. So I never hold back in worship because every time I come, a Beautiful Exchange takes place.

I come as I am…
…God comes as He is,
and we share our moment.

Why don't you take time now to stop and worship Jesus? Come as you are and enter into the Beautiful Exchange. As you give of yourself, allow God to pour all He is into you. Allow His presence to empower and strengthen you so you can go into your day filled and ready to face whatever challenges may come your way.

Chapter 5

Wonder Woman

So I have to admit to being a bit of a fan of superhero movies. There's something about a superhero arriving in all their prowess and saving the world from the evil villain. My family and I are big Marvel fans. We've watched all the movies several times. Much to my children's disgust, however, my favourite superhero is from the DC comics. You guessed it, Wonder Woman. You may be thinking that is so cliché and predictable! She's a woman, and you're a woman, so that's the only reason you like her. And yes, that's one reason I love Wonder Woman, but it's also a lot more.

Love at First Superhero

It all started back when I was a toddler. Now I know you may argue you can't remember anything when you're a toddler, but I have a couple of vivid memories. Like the time I travelled to Hawaii as a two-year-old.

My sister and I hula danced with leis around our necks, and all the tourists around us were remarking on how cute we were.

I also remember being in the Royal Brisbane Hospital as a toddler. It was Ekka time, and for some reason, I can remember standing at the hospital window and looking out at Side Show Alley. For those non-Brisbanites, the Ekka is short for exhibition (in Australia, we love to shorten our words). The Ekka is like a big carnival, with shows, rides, parades and all sorts of displays. They sell show bags full of lollies, chocolates and toys, which is a kid's delight! Anyway, this particular year, my Dad and sister went to the Ekka. I couldn't go because I was sick in hospital, so my Dad and sister brought me back a show bag. It was the Wonder Woman show bag. From that moment, it was love at first superhero!

As you can imagine, when the Wonder Woman movie came out in 2017 starring Gal Gadot I was all in. I went to see it with my husband, and it didn't disappoint. I've seen it several times since and must admit there are some far-fetched scenes, and some of the special effects looked totally unrealistic. Despite this, I still love the movie, and certain scenes always challenge and move me. Yes, I pretty much cry every time I see this film.

There is one scene in particular that always stirs me and makes me cry. It is the scene where Steve, Diana, and some of the men working for Steve travel to the front. They are walking through the trenches. It is Diana's first encounter with the war, and she is horrified by the grotesqueness and atrocities of war. The script reads like this:

"***DIANA:*** *(to Steve) We need to help these people.*

Steve looks across no man's land, shakes his head.

STEVE: *We need to stay on mission.*

THE CHIEF: *(nods to Steve) And there's no safe crossing for at least a day ahead.*

CHARLIE: *Then what are we waitin' for?*

DIANA: *But these people are dying, they've nothing to eat. And in the village... Enslaved, she said. Women. Children.*

STEVE: *There's nothing we can do about that.*

DIANA: *How can you say that? What is the matter with you?*

STEVE: *This is no man's land, Diana. It means no man can cross it. This is the worst point on the entire front. This battalion has been here for nearly a year, and they've barely gained an inch because on the other side are Germany's deadliest soldiers. Pointing machine guns at every square inch of this place. This is not something you can cross. It's not possible.*

DIANA: *So we do nothing?*

STEVE: *We are doing something. We can't save every person in this war. Besides, it's not what we came here to do.*

(She steps away from the group, turning away from them. Steve thinks she's upset. But when Diana turns back to Steve, he sees her face of determination, wearing ANTIOPE'S TIARA – AND FOR THE FIRST TIME – WE REALLY SEE WONDER WOMAN!)

DIANA: *No, but it's what I'm going to do.*

Diana moves past the team, stepping over the top of the trench.

***STEVE:** DIANA, NO!!!*"[3]

We all know what happens next…

…She walks out onto No Man's Land, and a bullet comes flying through the air. She lifts her arm, and it deflects off her armour. She begins running and deflecting one bullet after the next, and suddenly, all the men realise they can win the battle and come out to join her.

Do I have the Courage to Step into No Man's Land?

I can't help but be moved and inspired by such a dialogue. Most women would agree they felt their inner 'Wonder Woman' rise up within them when they watched that scene. I was no different, as I caught myself whispering, "I want to be that! I want to be that strong, brave, courageous woman, for my family, for those around me, for me." But in reality, more often than not, I'm like the people stuck in the trenches, afraid, despondent, giving up hope I could ever affect change. I mean, that's what everybody keeps telling me, right? They say, "It's not possible." They say, "It's always been like this," or "This is the way things are these days – you can't fight it." Even when I ask why nobody is doing anything? I'm not brave enough to climb the ladder. Who am I kidding? I'm no superhero.

What gave Diana the courage to step out onto the battlefield while bullets were fired straight at her? You might be saying, "Duh! She had superpowers." But until that moment, she hadn't known how to wield those powers. She could only wield them effectively when she understood her true identity and came into the knowledge of who she was.

---

[3] *Wonder Woman*, Patty Jenkins, featuring Gal Gadot, Chris Pine, Robin Wright, Danny Hutson, David Thewlis, Connie Nielsen, Elena Anaya, Warner Bros. Pictures, 2017, Motion Picture, 2017.

Suddenly it hits me. No, I'm no superhero, but I am a child of the resurrected King, and being brave and having the courage to be a spiritual Wonder Woman has nothing to do with me and my abilities or strength. It's all about Him and what He did for me.

In ***Ephesians 2:4-10 (TPT)*** it says,

But God still loved us with such great love. He is so rich in compassion and mercy. Even when we were dead and doomed in our many sins, he united us into the very life of Christ and saved us by his wonderful grace! He raised us up with Christ the exalted One, and we ascended with him into the glorious perfection and authority of the Heavenly realm, for we are now co-seated as one with Christ! Throughout the coming ages we will be the visible display of the infinite, limitless riches of his grace and kindness, which was showered upon us in Jesus Christ. For it was only through this wonderful grace that we believed in him. Nothing we did could ever earn this salvation, for it was the gracious gift from God that brought us to Christ! So no one will ever be able to boast, for salvation is never a reward for good works or human striving. (I LOVE THIS PART SO MUCH!) We have become his poetry, a re-created people that will fulfill the destiny he has given each of us, for we are joined to Jesus, the Anointed One. Even before we were born, God planned in advance our destiny and the good works we would do to fulfill it!

And in ***Romans 8:37-39 (TPT)*** it says,

Yet even in the midst of all these things, we triumph over them all, for God has made us to be more than conquerors, and his demonstrated love is our glorious victory over everything! So now I live with the confidence that there is nothing in the universe with the power to separate us from God's love. I'm convinced that his love will triumph over death, life's troubles, fallen angels, or dark rulers in the Heavens. There is nothing in our present or future circumstances that can weaken his love. There is no power above us or beneath us – no power that could ever be found in the universe that can distance us from God's passionate love, which is lavished upon us through our Lord Jesus, the Anointed One!

There is a lost world out there – people who need saving. And yes, we may have to cross No Man's Land to reach them, but every soul is worth fighting for. Just as at one time, our soul was worth fighting for. However, we will never reach the one if we try to do it in human strength and ability.

Before we take up the cause and climb that ladder, we must know who we are in Christ. It's so easy to let each passing day diminish our salvation. We might wake up in the morning and throw out a "Thank you, Jesus, for dying for me" and then move on to the next thing. However, we need to approach our everyday lives with a renewed revelation of what Christ has done for us and who we are in Him, so when we are called to go fight for the one, we are not shrinking back saying, "There's nothing we can do, we can't save everyone." No! We climb that ladder, and we say, "No, we can't, but He can, and I chose to fight with Him."

Be a Lioness! Fight for Your Children at All Costs

I can't help but stress the importance of this when it comes to our children. I would be remiss as a mother if I didn't talk about being a Christian Mum at some point in this book. I will preface this by saying I'm not a parenting expert or a child psychologist. Nor have I had a perfect record as a Mum. I've made mistakes, and so have my kids. So I'm not going to get all 'judgey' and start telling you the dos and don'ts of Christian parenting. Instead, I am going to share my heart.

You see, even though I grew up in a Christian home and now my children are being brought up in a Christian home, it doesn't guarantee immunity from difficulties. There is a world out there that we live in, and our children live in it too. So at some point, you will, not might, you will face situations that will challenge your beliefs. Likely your children will try to rebel and want to go against your wishes deliberately. It can be on something small, like watching a movie at a friend's house they know you would disapprove of them watching. To bigger issues that can get truly messy.

So how do we deal with this? Well, there is no one pill fixes all solution, but I will say one thing, and it might be some of the best advice you will ever hear. When it comes to your children, don't accept the status quo. Well, of course not, Andrina! No one wants their child to be mediocre. However, I'm not talking about mediocrity. I'm not even talking about our children's behaviour or the choices they make. I'm talking about the choices we as parents make in response to our children's behaviour and choices.

One too many times, I've been on the receiving end of this phrase, "This is what every young person does these days. It's normal." And my response is typical, "I know. What can you do?" Talk about being a coward and sitting down in the muddy trenches of life and accepting defeat!" In all honesty, that's what my mouth is saying out loud because I know that's what people want to hear. Inside, however, I'm having a Wonder Woman moment because deep down in my spirit, I know that I can't just do nothing.

Our children will choose their own paths, and these might not always be the paths that follow God's ways. We cannot stop them, and we can't force them to follow God, but that doesn't mean we accept it.

We can, however, do the one thing no one else in this world will do for our children, and that's to be their Wonder Woman. We need to fight for them.

We are pretty good at doing this naturally, but we also need to do this in a spiritual sense. We all probably have stories of praying grandmothers and mothers who went into spiritual battle for us when we were young. I know my Mum still prays earnestly for her grandchildren, but now is the time for the baton to pass to me. It's my turn to rise up and go into a spiritual battle for my kids.

1 Peter 5:8 (NIV) says,

Be alert and of sober mind. Your enemy the devil prowls around like a roaring lion looking for someone to devour.

If an actual lion somehow got into your home and tried to devour your children, I know you would do everything in your power to stop that lion and save your kids. Yet the devil is roaming around like a spiritual lion, and we seem to sit back and let him take our kids without battering our eyelids. In fact, all too often, I think we are utterly oblivious to what he is doing. So what exactly should we be doing to fight for our kids?

It's Time to Go to the Mattresses

For want of using another movie reference…

I've never watched a Godfather movie in my life, and probably not many women have. However, we all know what this phrase means, cos just about every woman from my vintage has watched 'You've Got Mail' with Meg Ryan and Tom Hanks, and we all know what 'Go the the Mattresses' means, right? FIGHT!!

In *Ephesians 6:10-18 (NIV)* it says,

Finally, be strong in the Lord and in his mighty power. Put on the full armour of God, so that you can take your stand against the devil's schemes. For our struggle is not against flesh and blood, but against the rulers, against the authorities, against the powers of this dark world and against the spiritual forces of evil in the Heavenly realms. Therefore put on the full armour of God, so that when the day of evil comes, you may be able to stand your ground, and after you have done everything, to stand. Stand firm then, with the belt of truth buckled around your waist, with the breastplate of righteousness in place, and with your feet fitted with the readiness that comes from the gospel of peace. In addition to all this, take up the shield of faith, with which you can extinguish all the flaming arrows of the evil one. Take the helmet of salvation and the sword of the Spirit, which is the word of God. And pray in the Spirit on all occasions with all kinds of prayers and requests. With this in mind, be alert and always keep on praying for all the Lord's people.

Let's break this down:

'And after you have done everything, to stand. Stand firm'

Firstly, we need to stand and not wavier in our convictions. Even if everyone is telling us otherwise, we need to keep taking our stand. It doesn't mean being haughty and acting like we are better than others. There is no place for religiosity in this battle. However, the Bible tells us that although we live in the world, we are not of the world. We are different, and despite popular belief, if the Bible tells us to be different, then it is absolutely possible for our kids and us to do so. When you feel like you have done everything to stand, KEEP STANDING. Don't bow to pressure.

I have long resigned myself to the fact I am not my children's friend. Nor am I the 'cool Mum' or the Mum who lets them do whatever they want. What I am is the Mother who loves them, and will stand for and with them. I will fight for them, both in the natural and in the spiritual. Come to think of it, that kinda makes me a pretty cool Mum.

'Therefore put on the full armour of God, so that when the day of evil comes, you may be able to stand your ground.'

If you are going to take a stand for your children, then you need to be equipped. Wonder Woman didn't stand in the middle of the battle looking beautiful, even though she was stunningly so. No, she had full use of the weapons her mother had given her. We, too, have been given a full array of armour that we all too often leave at home. We can't adequately fight the battle if we are ill-equipped. So let's take a closer look at our God-given armour and the power it wields.

'Stand firm then, with the belt of truth buckled around your waist'

Truth is a quality we see little of in the world today. Thanks to the digital age, the facts are only one google search away, and our social media feeds are riddled with opinions. Truth, on the other hand, is a rare commodity. So when our children search for this, where will they go looking and what will they find?

Our homes must be a safe space for truth. When it comes to truth, the best place to find it is in the Word of God. When you don't have all the answers to the tricky questions that your kids will ask you, or when you have to decide what's best for your child, there is no better place to go than the Word of God.

It's interesting that in this passage, the truth comes first and is likened to a belt around our waist, the centre of our body. To me, this signifies the importance of the truth of God's Word being central in all we do. Truth should be the first thing we run to in all circumstances. Our kids need to see us reading our Bibles and hear us speaking scriptures over our family. It needs to be as natural as breathing. That way, when they face challenges and difficult decisions, their default will be the truth.

'With the breastplate of righteousness in place'

The dictionary defines righteousness as *'the quality of being morally right or justifiable'*. Again this is another quality that is rare in our modern world today. We live in a world where everything is grey, and boundaries are a thing of the past. However, in this passage, righteousness is compared to the breastplate. The piece of armour that protects our heart. As a Mum, I want my children's hearts to be protected. I want them to know right from wrong and be confident of this despite living in a world of blurred boundaries. So along the way, as they grow, I need to teach them and show them how to walk in righteousness. The challenge in all this is to do it out of love and not fear. Teach them that righteousness is good and the benefits are wonderful. People are often afraid to become Christians because of all the rules they think they have to follow. When you hear the word righteousness, you can easily equate it to following rules. However, that is not how God sees righteousness at all.

Let me give you an illustration: Imagine you have moved into your dream home, and you are unpacking all your boxes. In your new home, you have a photoshoot worthy designer kitchen full of cupboards and endless storage. Now, most people would unpack their boxes and fill the cabinets to enjoy their fabulous kitchen. Not me!! I don't want to be confined by all these cupboards – I want to be free and go with my mood. So I'm not going to put away all my things. I'm going to let them lie all over my counter space and see where this takes me. I know what you're all saying right now. "Are you crazy? You can't possibly live like that!" Yet many people live their lives like this because they don't want to be bound by rules, but that's religion, not righteousness.

Righteousness is very much like a designer kitchen. God has given us a beautiful gift called righteousness that enables us to put all of our life inside it. Its purpose is not to disable us like we often think, but rather to allow us to utilise what we have to the best of our ability. I can't use my designer kitchen properly if I don't put my stuff away. I'm unable to use the space to its fullest potential.

Righteousness is the same. Yes, it gives us boundaries, but not to bind and restrict. It provides us with the freedom to enjoy all God has for us. To me, this is how we need to paint righteousness in our homes. It protects our hearts, enabling us to live in the complete freedom Christ has given us.

'And with your feet fitted with the readiness that comes from the gospel of peace.'

Who knows family life can be far from peaceful? Most parents would use words like hectic or chaotic, but very rarely, when referring to a house full of kids, would you use the word peace. Notice this verse says, *'feet fitted with the readiness that comes from the gospel of peace.'* Yet again, God's word is central. His word brings peace, and peace brings readiness. Let me tell you when you're a parent, you certainly have to be ready! Ready for anything because curveballs are going to come flying. You have to have those shoes on ready to go at any moment. I love that readiness comes from peace. I love that if I fill my home with God's gospel, it will be peaceful, and I will be ready for whatever comes.

My daughter plays worship music every night when she sleeps. She has been doing it since she was a young child. Every night she plays the same album by Kelli Copeland. It is a combination of old hymns and scriptures spoken over music. It plays all night on repeat. One morning as I woke and could hear the music playing, God spoke to me about it. This is what I wrote that morning as God spoke to me:

> *"This morning, when I woke Lainie up, she looked so peaceful. I could hear softly playing beside her head the Kelli Copeland worship and scriptures album we used to play when she was little. She's been playing it every night lately. At that moment this morning, God showed me how powerful it is, what's she's doing. That it is a hedge of favour & protection around her, and it is like a balm that is keeping her for God's purposes and plan. He told me He has set her apart to be a point of difference in this world. He also said there is an overflow blessing for our whole family because even though the scriptures play softly in her room all night, it is flowing out and blessing our whole household. God sees what she is doing in the secret place. He sees that it is authentic and genuine, and His plan for our Lainie is very special. Praise God! He hears the prayers of a Mum and brings peace and promise!"*

I don't think any other words could illustrate this any better! Peace comes through His Word, and it equips our entire household to be ready.

'In addition to all this, take up the shield of faith, with which you can extinguish all the flaming arrows of the evil one.'

Wow, that's a bold statement!! In addition to truth, righteousness and peace take up faith – that will extinguish ALL of the devil's flaming arrows. In ancient times, shields were similar to a large door, made from two layers of wood, covered with flame-resistant material. When the flaming arrow hit the shield, it would extinguish it before it penetrated the shield. Faith, like the shield, is an impenetrable force. None of the enemy's attempts to attack can withstand the power of faith. So how do we walk this out and model faith for our children?

First, we come back to what I've said before, God is at the centre of everything. Faith is total reliance upon God, and we can't do this if God isn't the centre of our homes. We have to walk this out for our children to see – faith being outworked every day in every circumstance. Faith won't always look the same. Faith can be loud and bold, triumphant and audacious. Faith can also be quiet, barely a whisper – a calm trust that He will work it all for good. Faith can just be! It is something we hold onto and lean into in everyday, ordinary tasks. However it looks, faith is something we should always have.

That doesn't mean it's always easy to have faith. Life can wear our faith down, and there can be times when it can seem like faith is one big, fat joke! But remember, the author of Ephesians urges us to stand and keep standing. So even if faith seems like the slightest flicker, don't relent, don't get tired and drop your shield. It is your cover and protection for you, your family and your home. Keep your faith in God. Never give up!

'Take the helmet of salvation'

As I write this, it's December. The season where we reflect on God's gift of salvation to humankind. Yet, it all began way back in the Garden of Eden. God's heart for salvation was present right from the beginning of time. It's easy to think about the Old Testament as all about the Law, but when you read it through the eyes of grace, you can see salvation woven amongst the pages from Genesis through to Malachi. It's a beautiful story about how much God loved us. About the outworking of that love from the beginning of time until now. I love the way the author of The Passion Translation describes it in ***Ephesians 1:9-10:***

And through the revelation of the Anointed One, he unveiled his secret desires to us—the hidden mystery of his long-range plan, which he was delighted to implement from the very beginning of time. And because of God's unfailing purpose, this detailed plan will reign supreme through every period of time until the fulfilment of all the ages finally reaches its climax – when God makes all things new in all of Heaven and earth through Jesus Christ.

Just as the breastplate of righteousness protects our heart, the helmet of salvation protects our mind. Our mind is renewed when we meditate on God's love and redemption. I don't know about you, but I feel refreshed and renewed when I read the verse above. I feel strengthened by the words that speak of God's plan for me from the beginning of time. I feel wrapped in a blanket of love and wholeness. This is salvation!

In western society, mental health issues are prevalent and are ever on the rise, particularly amongst our young people. There is much talk about health for our body and mind. How wonderful is our God! He knew good mental health was fundamental for our wellbeing, and He gave us a weapon to combat it – Salvation! Learn to meditate upon your salvation. Teach your children to meditate upon their salvation. Your mind, health, family, home, workplace, and the world around you will be all the better for it.

'And the sword of the Spirit, which is the word of God.'

Interestingly, out of all the armour described in these verses, the sword is the only attacking piece of armour. What does this tell us about the Word of God? It tells us that the Bible is not just something we read and meditate on. It should be used to take ground and advance God's kingdom. So how do we actively use God's Word? By declaring it aloud over our lives and over our families' lives. We should be speaking God's

Word aloud in our homes. Our children should be hearing us declare God's Word. God values His Word so much. Listen to what he tells the children of Israel about his Word in **Deuteronomy 11:18-21 (NIV)**

Fix these words of mine in your hearts and minds; tie them as symbols on your hands and bind them on your foreheads. Teach them to your children, talking about them when you sit at home and when you walk along the road, when you lie down and when you get up. Write them on the doorframes of your houses and on your gates, so that your days and the days of your children may be many in the land the Lord swore to give your ancestors, as many as the days that the Heavens are above the earth.

God was saying to the children of Israel, and He is saying to us today. "I want my words to encompass every part of your life. I want them to be so natural to you that it's like breathing. I want you to teach them to your children, so they will know their power and the blessings they bring."

Today the Word of God is a powerful weapon. Yet, so often, we are not using it to its full potential. It's time to be proactive and start speaking out the Word of God more and more over our lives. In *Hebrews 4:12*, it refers to being sharper than a doubled-edged sword. One edge to bring down the forces of darkness and the other edge to bring the promises of God's blessing to fulfilment.

'And pray in the Spirit on all occasions with all kinds of prayers and requests. With this in mind, be alert and always keep on praying for all the Lord's people.'

As a family, we pray together each evening before bed. As part of our prayer time, we always put on the armour of God. It is something I did growing up and have kept doing with my children. We keep it very simple so that we can say it together, and when we get to this part of the passage, we say, "We pray in all we do." I love this concept of prayer – pray in everything. To me, prayer should be just that, talking to God about everything in our lives. We should be able to pray wherever we go and about all things. At times we can get religious about praying, and it shouldn't be this way. Prayer is something we can all do.

The above is how I think about prayer and try to model it for my children. I have a close relationship with my Father God. I also have a close relationship with my husband and children. I talk to them about everything – the happy, the sad, the silly, and the serious, what annoys me and what I love. I talk to them all the time. So why should it be any different when I speak to God? I don't just pray when I need something, but I chat with God. I tell him when I'm feeling upset about something, or I'm disappointed, I tell Him I'm thankful when something has gone my way. I talk to Him about things that other people might think are silly, like how much I love strawberries or trees. I tell Him when I feel something is unfair or I need a hug. I ask Him to help me find a carpark, and I ask Him to help me with my relationships, work, study, and life. Why? Because He's my Heavenly Father, and to me, that's what *'pray in everything means.'*

When I consider prayer this way, it's no longer weird because it seems perfectly normal and natural to me. Unfortunately, we can get caught up in the dos and don'ts of how to pray, which can put our kids off wanting to pray. I don't want that for my kids or other young people. I want them to learn that praying is natural, and it doesn't have to be fancy because it's a conversation with the closest person in our lives.

Today, let's rise up, fully equipped with the armour God has given us, and begin to fight for our children like never before. Let's be godly superheroes who will stop at nothing to demonstrate how to live for Jesus in this dark world.

Being a superhero for God doesn't mean you will be immune to trials and challenges. That's why God has equipped us with His armour to be ready for any challenge and season. In our Christian walk, there will be many seasons. Seasons of triumph and celebration, seasons of heartache and disappointment. Seasons when it seems like not a great deal is happening at all and seasons of waiting. The next part of this book talks about these seasons and encourages us to remain steadfast to God whatever the season we may be in.

Chapter 6

My Tree Obsession

I love trees! I am quite obsessed with them. There is something about trees that makes me go all deep and philosophical. A few years ago, we moved to a beautiful five-acre property. It's full of trees – beautiful, Australian gum trees. Every morning I sit on my couch with a coffee in hand and look out my back window at all the trees in our yard. They are so grand and majestic, and it makes me feel grounded. Every morning I say the same thing in my mind, "Wow, God! You loved me so much that you brought our family to this beautiful property to live amongst all these breathtaking trees because you knew how much I love trees."

There is so much we can learn from trees. In fact, there are many references in the Bible to trees. One of my favourite verses is found in ***Psalm 1:1-3 (NKJV)***

Blessed is the man who walks not in the counsel of the ungodly, nor stands in the path of sinners, nor sits in the seat of the scornful; But his delight is in the law of the Lord, and in His law he meditates day and night. He shall be like a tree planted by the rivers of water, that brings forth its fruit in its season, whose leaf also shall not wither; And whatever he does shall prosper.

Psalm 104:16-17 (TPT) is another beautiful verse about trees:

The trees of the Lord drink until they're satisfied. Lebanon's lofty trees stand tall right where you planted them. Within their branches you provide for birds a place to build their nests; even herons find a home in the cypress trees.

I'm also a big believer that God uses creation to speak to us. I don't think God created the earth, and then that was the end of creation's role in echoing the voice of Heaven. I believe God is constantly speaking in and through creation, and we only need to quiet ourselves, look and listen, and we will see and hear from God. As part of an artist is reflected in their artwork, so too, the heart of our Creator is reflected in His creation. Yes, humankind was made in the image of God, but God created the whole universe. Therefore, it should come as no surprise when we see Him in creation. I think we often take that for granted and miss some profound truths. God is in the trees and the flowers. God is in the mountains and the seas. He's in the elements, and He's in the creatures on the earth. So let's lean in for a moment and let the trees speak.

I Feel PURPLE!

One of my favourite trees is the Jacaranda tree. Jacaranda trees are famous for their beautiful lilac blooms that cover their branches in

Spring. All over Brisbane from late September through October, these trees are in bloom, and it is quite a magnificent sight to see. In some parts of Brisbane, if you drive up a hill, you can look out and see a patchwork of purple all over the city. My Mum loves Jacarandas, and she'll grab whoever she can and take them for a drive all over Brisbane, Jacaranda spotting. At some point, she'll find one that is particularly majestic, park under it, then make whoever is in the car with her get out, stand under the tree and shout, "I feel purple! I feel purple!"

I remember when I was a young student at university. My uni campus had so many Jacaranda trees, and they would start to bloom just before the end of year finals. We would always say, "If you hadn't started studying by the time the Jacarandas were in bloom, then you were in big trouble." I probably didn't enjoy the Jacarandas so much back then, but these days I can really enjoy them when it's Jacaranda season.

One day, I drove past a beautiful Jacaranda tree in bloom. I briefly admired the tree in all its glory but then suddenly realised I had driven past that tree all year and never noticed it until now. I thought about how the purple blooms would fade in a few weeks, and the tree would go back to being an ordinary tree. However, I realised what appears to be ordinary is, in fact, extraordinary. I began to admire the roots of this tree that are never seen but are working hard under the surface to nourish the tree so the whole tree can grow and blossom. I saw beauty in the trunk and branches that have toiled and weathered the seasons to be strong and faithful to allow the flowers to bloom in their time.

I thought about life and how it is a lot like the Jacaranda tree. There are moments in life where we bloom and celebrate the beauty of our successes. However, beyond this, there are many ordinary days. Days and moments may go unnoticed by those around us, but these days are indeed more beautiful than those days when we display stunning flowers. Through these seemingly ordinary days, our roots are growing deep to nourish us. Our trunk and branches are growing strong and weathering the seasons to support the beautiful blossoms that will surely come. So don't despise the days when there are no flowers in bloom, for those days are the making of beauty – they are the making of something spectacular. They are the days that don't just produce flowers but a lasting tree for generations to come.

As **Psalm 92:12-14 (NKJV)** says:

The righteous shall flourish like a palm tree. He shall grow like a cedar in Lebanon. Those who are planted in the house of the Lord shall flourish in the courts of our God. They shall still bear fruit in old age; They shall be fresh and flourishing.

And **Mark 4:30-32 (NKJV)**

Then He said, "To what shall we liken the kingdom of God? Or with what parable shall we picture it? It is like a mustard seed which, when it is sown on the ground, is smaller than all the seeds on earth; but when it is sown, it grows up and becomes greater than all herbs, and shoots out large branches, so that the birds of the air may nest under its shade."

Magnificence Takes Time

About a year later, I drove past this same tree. It was Jacaranda season again, and the tree was in bloom. I smiled as I thought about what God had placed in my heart a year ago, and I reflected on how much my heart had grown since then and the journey I had walked.

As I was thinking about these things, God began to whisper to me again. He spoke to me about how it takes years for the Jacaranda tree to transform from a tiny seed into a spectacular, blossoming tree. Patience isn't one of my strengths, so the thought of something taking years to reach its full potential doesn't excite me. Yet, that is how God works. He's a God of time and seasons. He's a skilled novelist who loves to pen dramatic plots with twists and turns and poignant moments, all precisely crafted into a magnificent story. So every year that passes, every season we travel, our story is unfolding. Our tree is growing. The roots are going deeper, the branches are becoming more robust and can hold more blooms. So with Him, we get better with time.

It is true for so many characters from the Bible. Joseph is a classic example of this. His brothers tossed him in a well and left him for dead. He then finds himself as a servant in a wealthy man's house, but that turns sour when the man's his wife tries to seduce him. Even though he does the right thing, he ends up in jail. While in prison, he meets two servants of Pharaoh and interprets their dreams. Still, it isn't until years later that he has the opportunity to go before Pharaoh and interpret his dream, which results in his promotion to second in charge in all of the land!

What about Moses? He went from a basket in the river Nile to Pharaoh's son, only to run away to the wilderness because he murdered an Egyptian. He spent forty years in the wilderness tending sheep, and while he was as far away from his destiny as he could have imagined, God showed up, and well, the rest is history.

Then there's Peter, Jesus' disciple. Well, he never seemed to get it right. He was always saying the wrong thing. Even after being Jesus' disciple for three years, he couldn't use self-control. He cut off a soldier's ear and then denied Jesus not once but three times! Despite all this, at just the right moment after waiting for fifty days in Jerusalem, he was anointed with the Holy Spirit and saw thousands of people saved in one day. After a lifetime of always saying the wrong thing, God used him to say exactly what needed to be said.

The Bible is full of these stories. Right throughout history, God has been doing the same thing. Unfortunately, today in our post-modern culture, we are used to everything being instant. Fast food, instant coffee, uber eats, online shopping with same-day delivery, Netflix, and social media – need I go on? In this digital age, everything is literally at our fingertips. If I want something, I google it, and there it is. And so, we've become the generation that can't wait for anything. However, who knows all good things come to those who wait?

Celebrate Every Year Lived and the Beauty of a Life Lived Well

This may come as a surprise but, do you know what? There is joy in the waiting. There's fun to be had along the way. God doesn't want us to suffer along the way and live our entire lives in misery, all for the prize at the end. That's why like the Jacaranda tree, we bloom in season. Sometimes the bloom will be small, but each year as we grow, it gets bigger and more majestic. So we need to learn to enjoy the journey, treasure each bloom, and not despise the future – because the future is definitely brighter and better!

My great Aunty passed away at the age of 103. About six months before she passed away, she went to the hospital. It was her first visit to hospital in 103 years – this so inspired me! I honestly think she epitomized the meaning of getting better with age. When she was 100, she flew on her own from Adelaide to Brisbane. She did not need to wear glasses or use a walking aid. I asked her if she still played the bagpipes, and she said, "No, just the electric chanter now." I asked her if she still danced, and she said, "No, but I sometimes do an Irish jig while I'm doing the dishes." Talk about living long and strong. What an inspiration!

My mere 44 years pales in comparison to 103, but sometimes I catch myself thinking, "I've missed my time, and I have nothing more to offer." Maybe you feel this way too. But imagine how boring life would be without the beautiful Jacaranda trees that bloom without fail every year, in celebration of another year lived. Yes, they are old, but they are stunningly beautiful! Young people are watching and looking for examples of lives lived long, and lives lived well. Teach your children to honour and respect their elders, but also to converse and listen to their tales of ages past.

So much can be learnt from age and wisdom. So don't be afraid to let yours shine. Regardless of your age or season in life, you are worthy, beautiful, and have much to give. So hold your head high, grey hairs and all! Be a majestic tree that inspires others. Remember, your tree is continuing to grow and bloom. Your story is still being written. You haven't reached the finale yet.

Let's turn our attention to a woman in the Bible who at first could not recognise the magnificence of her life lived well. In time, not only did she see the immense goodness in her life, but she was able to impart this into the lives of those around her.

Chapter 7

The Naomi Phenomenon

The world is full of everyday people doing normal kinds of stuff. Very few of us will reach celebrity status, stand on a platform or grace the cover of a magazine. It's easy in our western world to measure our lives based on being seen and thinking we have little significance because we live run of the mill lives. That is so depressing right there! Thank the Lord that doesn't have to be the sum of our existence.

As born-again believers living in the digital age of the 21st century, we can live normal lives with extraordinary impact. Yes, as a wife, mother, sister, friend, girl-boss, student, entrepreneur, whatever you do, you don't need a social media following of thousands. You don't even need a platform or a stage – you can be extraordinarily influential right where you are. In your home, office, school, university, whatever space you find yourself. The world desperately needs you! So hold onto your hats while I explain it further.

ANDRINA E. RIJKEN

And The Best Supporting Actress Goes To...

In the book of Ruth, the focus is very much on our heroine and her eventual betrothed, Boaz. But let's talk for a moment about our supporting actress Naomi. And oh, how she plays her role so well. In my opinion, she is absolutely fitting of an Oscar! What is so compelling about Naomi is she's a lot like me – a boring, middle-aged woman, and if you blink in the first few verses, you'll miss it. I've read Ruth many, many times, and it has never hit me. Not until I was in the process of translating the book of Ruth from Hebrew to English, verse by verse for a university course. Suddenly the story was being played out in slow motion. I began to look at things from Naomi's perspective and my life in recent years flashed before me. It all happened for me in verse 16 of chapter 1:

Ruth 1:16 (NLT)

But Ruth replied, "Don't ask me to leave you and turn back. Wherever you go, I will go; wherever you live, I will live. Your people will be my people, and your God will be my God.

Ruth saw something in Naomi that Naomi couldn't even see in herself. When Naomi looked in the mirror, she saw a woman who had become redundant, but when Ruth looked at Naomi, she saw the very woman she wanted to become. Ruth was so attracted to what Naomi had; she was willing to throw away all she knew to get some of what Naomi had. Naomi had lived life. She had married and raised two sons. She knew what it was to face hardship, pack up her family and move to a foreign land. She'd traversed the seasons of life and had come out with immense loss. Her heart was broken, and in her mind, she was merely an aged woman with nothing left to offer. She had served her time in

Moab and done so well, but now that season was over, and it was time to return to her promised land, not knowing how her future would unfold. And not knowing if she would be accepted and whether she would be able to contribute to her community.

While Naomi saw a woman passed her used by date with nothing that seemed of value, Ruth saw a woman to look up to and admire. A woman who had gone into a foreign land and had stayed faithful to her God, beliefs, values, morals, and convictions, never wavering even through the process of grief and loss. She saw a woman who had clung to her God through the most challenging of trials and never lost sight of her God's promises and love. Ruth saw a woman stand up for godly principles in a foreign land surround by false gods and wayward living. Yet, through it all, Naomi had remained faithful and true, and when it came time to leave, Ruth realised she wanted to be the woman she saw in Naomi.

I'll Have What She's Having

In **Ruth 1:16,** it says: *"Don't ask me to leave you and turn back."*

The Hebrew word used for 'turn back' is *mei ahairei*, which means *'from after or behind'*. Translated literally, Ruth said, "You will not urge me to leave you, to go back from after you."

In other words, she was following in Naomi's footsteps. Naomi was leaving a legacy that Ruth was following. Ruth was learning how to follow God as Naomi lived out her life. Without Naomi realising, she was the light of salvation, pointing Ruth toward the one true God. Naomi lived a life true to God. She thought it didn't amount to much and that she was insignificant, but Ruth was drawn to it. So much so, she literally clung to Naomi and would not let her go.

Ultimately Ruth would marry Boaz, and they would have a son named Jesse, the father of King David, the very lineage of our Saviour, Jesus. Naomi was remarkable and incredibly influential, and she didn't even know it! Naomi didn't realise that by simply living a seemingly ordinary, unsuspecting, 'boring' life for God, she was instrumental in the big plan of salvation for the whole world.

God Always Rewards Faithfulness

As the book of Ruth comes to a close, listen to what it says in **Ruth 4:13-17 (The Voice)**

Then Boaz took responsibility of Ruth, and they married. After they came together, Ruth conceived by the Eternal's provision, and later she gave birth to a son.

Women (to Naomi): Praise the Eternal One. He has not abandoned you. He did not leave you without a redeeming guardian. May your offspring become famous all through Israel. May this child give you a new life. May he strengthen you and provide for you in your old age. Look at your daughter-in-law, Ruth. She loves you. This one devoted daughter is better to you than seven sons would be. She is the one who gave you this child.

Then Naomi held the child tightly in her arms and cared for him. All around her, friends cried out, "Naomi has a son!" They named the child Obed because he would provide for his grandmother. Obed grew up and became the father of Jesse. Jesse, too, became a father one day, the father of David.

Notice in verse 17 the women of the town say, "Naomi has a son!" In the end, it's Naomi, not Ruth, who receives the credit. Why is that?

Well, I believe God was rewarding Naomi for her faithfulness to Him. He was saying,

> *"My beautiful daughter! You have been so faithful to me. I've seen the way you've followed me all the days of your life, even when you thought no one noticed. I saw. I knew. And now I'm rewarding you for your faithful love and devotion to me. You'll never know the full extent of how your faithfulness and integrity has influenced the course of history or how it has made way for my perfect plan of salvation. Day in day out, you have stayed true to my ways. In the big and small, when others thought it didn't matter. When no one was looking, and when there was no recognition, you were unwavering in your commitment to me. So, mark my words because of what you have done, thousands of years on, they will still be reading about it. Bless you, my beautiful daughter! You have thought your life of insignificance has mattered little, but your devotion to me has mattered a great deal! Well done, my child!"*

Today God is saying the same to you! We have to remind ourselves that God doesn't miss a single moment of our lives, and he will always reward his faithful children.

A Return to Fullness

Remember how in **Ruth 1:21**, when Naomi returned to Bethlehem, she told the people, *"I left full, but I have returned empty."* Well, listen to what it says in **Ruth Chapter 3:17 (NKJV)**

> *And she said, "These six ephahs of barley he gave me; for he said to me. "Do not go empty-handed to your mother-in-law."*

What a beautiful picture of the Father's redemptive goodness returning to us! Sometimes we can feel we have been stripped of all fullness, but when we least expect it, there is always a return to the fullness of God.

As a 44-year-old wife and mother, I have lived life, and yes, I still have plenty of living to do. But, as time passes, you learn life isn't always how you imagined it would be. Things you thought would be certain were not. Seasons change, hurt and disappointment come. You move homes, change jobs, meet new people, all sorts of things. Your hair starts to go grey. Wrinkles appear – you're desperately trying to hold on to your youth. And then one day, you start looking at yourself in the mirror, and you begin asking, "Who am I? How did I get to this? Is this really going to be my life? I thought I should have amounted to more than this, but I'm just ordinary. I'm just Little Miss Boring!"

And so, the pity party goes until you shake it off and get on with your day. And you're okay for a while, but one morning it happens again and again. Disappointment has made a home in your heart, and it's telling you your time is finished. It's telling you, you have nothing to offer anymore, you're old, you're nobody, why would anyone listen to you. But that's where disappointment is wrong. Cos, you've been clinging to God, and He's heard your every cry and plea. He's seen your every tear, and He knows your every dream. He's gently leading you into the Promised Land, and you may not be able to see it yet, but there's a generation coming behind you.

Like Naomi, you are remarkable and incredibly influential without even knowing it, and God is bringing back all the fullness and more into your house. They've been watching how you've lived through all the ups and downs of life, and they are chasing you down, clinging to you because without knowing it, you've been showing them how to live for God in a very dark world.

Be an Intentional Influencer

At first, Naomi was unaware of her influence, but as the story progresses, she realises Ruth is looking to her for direction. It's like she gets a new lease on life, a new purpose, a new vision, and Naomi becomes very intentional in how she guides Ruth.

Today there is a whole generation of *Ruths* in the world. They are crying out for role models and people to follow, often searching in all the wrong places and looking at images that are distorting their view of what is good and lovely. We need to be intentional about being *Naomis* in today's *Ruth generation*. Showing them what godly looks like and how to live a holy life and do it well – how to be uncompromising in our faith, beliefs and morals no matter what the world is saying, and how to live for God through the triumphs and disappointments.

Don't get me wrong, how thrilling would it be to stand on a stage and preach or lead worship in front of thousands, and I would never take away from the power and anointing in that. Still, God needs servants who will live for Him every day, shining the light, so those coming after us will be desperate to follow Him. Who are the *Ruths* in your life? It's our sons and daughters, our nieces and nephews, children we may teach, a neighbour, a young person at church, a colleague at work. They are everywhere.

Realise that no matter how young or old you are, you have influence no matter how known or unknown you are. Every day you have the power to influence someone, and you can choose what that influence will be. Choose for it to be the type of influence that will bring others into the kingdom of God. Choose to be a *Naomi* to the generations of *Ruths* coming behind you.

In her day, Naomi was God's plan to bring about salvation. Likewise, because of Jesus, we are God's plan for salvation in this modern world.

As boring as I think mine is at times, it is through our lives that people see Jesus!

Influence Others to Stand Out from the Crowd

Ruth 3:10-11 (The VOICE)

Boaz: May the Eternal bless you, my daughter, for the loyal love you are showing now is even greater than what you showed before. You have not pursued a younger man – either a rich one or a poor one. You may rest easy. You have nothing to fear, my child. I will do everything you ask. Everyone in this city agrees you are a woman of virtuous character.

I am completely blown away by these verses. Boaz speaks so highly of Ruth's virtuous character. As a mother, the resounding prayer for my children is that they will not be like everyone else, chasing after any man or woman that may come their way, but rather have hearts so pure that they set themselves apart for a godly man or woman. That they will be noticed and known, like Ruth, for their virtuosity and integrous character.

This passage speaks volumes about the example and influence that Naomi had on Ruth. Naomi was a Jew living in Moab – she was a foreigner. And Ruth was a Moabitess, not a Jew. So Ruth's gods, customs, and way of life were entirely different to Naomi's God, customs, and way of life. Yet, despite living in a foreign land, Naomi remained steadfast to her God, customs, and way of life.

This should ring true for how we live today as Christians in our modern society – we are in the world, but not of the world. We already know that Ruth chose to turn away from her way of life to follow after Naomi. Yet, what is so beautiful is there is no trace of her former way of living when she meets Boaz. She was completely transformed. She was no longer known at the city gate for being a Moabitess. Instead, it says, "Everyone in this city agrees you are a woman of virtuous character." Naomi had influenced Ruth so much that she had become a beautiful woman.

What a stunning picture of salvation! The old has gone, and the new has come. Naomi's influence was not because she was religious and pious. It came by humbly living out her life for God day by day. She showed Ruth that there was an alternative to how everyone else was doing it. She is the type of woman that as Christian women we should aspire to be, whether married or single, whether a mother or a grandmother, aunty or friend, whether famous or simply a regular, everyday person.

I guess this is the part in the book where I talk about my love-hate relationship with social media. Look, it was bound to come up, and now is as good a time as any. I love, love love how we can connect with people so easily – relatives and friends who may not live nearby. I love catching up on all their news, and I can say I am genuinely happy about all the great things happening in people's lives. I love being able to joke with cousins, see what my school friends are doing these days, and keeping in touch with people I've worked with, done church with, etc. BUT…. And it's a big BUT (😊😊😊 – sorry I have a son, and he thinks it's hilarious when I say the word 'but/butt' – it's a boy thing) I immensely dislike that there are no limits to when, where, what, how and why we post. In essence, today's society has no filters, and that concerns me. Unfortunately, our children are growing up in a culture of no filters.

I struggle with how everything is so sexualised, especially photos young girls post on social media, thinking it's completely innocent and normal. I'm not talking about nude selfies here. I'm talking about the shots where they're fully clothed, but they pose to accentuate certain parts of their bodies. I see these shots all over social media feeds, and I'm horrified, but then I second guess myself and think things like, "Well, aren't you a prude!"

However, when I read Ruth 3:10, where Boaz commends Ruth for being virtuous and not chasing after men, I'm like, "Yes! This is my heart! This is what I want for my children! They do not have to be like everyone else. They can set themselves apart for God, and the Bible promises in His perfect timing, their integrity will stand out and be noticed!" Wow! I'm jumping up and down, cheering about this.

The other day I read this quote by Alex Seely on Instagram, *"In this generation, the way a Christian will stand out is by doing EVERYTHING OPPOSITE to what the culture is doing."* Yep – I was jumping and shouting at that one too. As a Mum, I've had many internal battles about how to parent our children. Peer pressure is not just something our kids are facing these days. It's just as real for Mums and Dads out there. In this age of freedom of speech, there are so many voices screaming at us. Trying to tell us how we should be living. Interestingly, the message is, "Do, be and act how you want to." No one can judge you for being who you want to be (Ironically, I believe we live in the most judgmental society of all times). But underlying all this is a message that is not liberating at all if you think otherwise.

As a Christian parent, I have often wondered if I am too strict, too harsh, too old-fashioned, or too restrictive. If I use the world's viewpoint as my moral compass, then the answer is a resounding yes!! But I'm not one to do that. You see, my true north has always been the Word of God, and what His Word says is very counter-culture, but I've never been one to follow a trend. And lately, my motto for myself and my family has been, 'We are meant to be distinctively different.' Not in a pious way that sets us apart as being better than others, but in a way that is so unique that when people encounter our family, they admire it and are drawn to it. It's not about being attracted to me but rather about being drawn to God. This is what the underlying theme of the book of Ruth is all about.

Don't Go It Alone

When Naomi returned to Bethlehem, she was so negative about herself. So much so that she told everyone to call her *'Mara'*, which means bitter. Wow! She was really jaded by life. If I'm honest, though, I'm not constantly overflowing with positivity about myself. I can have days where I'm not feeling it, and it can make me feel rotten. What I love about the book of Ruth is that the whole community gets involved in the story (Side note: seriously, someone needs to make this into a Broadway musical).

We read about the town's women and the men/elders at the gate, throughout the story. In Naomi's case, the people who come around her when she returns from Moab help change her mindset. She's kinda Captain Grumpy Pants when she returns and doesn't seem to rate Ruth at all. Talk about harsh! Ruth has thrown herself at Naomi, and Naomi doesn't even give her a look in when they return to Bethlehem. But the people of the town are so excited to see her. As they gather around and welcome her back, her spirit begins to lift, and she begins to get a new vision and purpose for life.

From chapter 2 in the book of Ruth, we begin to see things turn around for Naomi and Ruth. To me, this resembles the modern-day church and signifies the importance of being planted in the house. When life gets hard, and we've lost our joy, it's the love, support, and encouragement from our church family that can be what we need to keep going. I would be lost without my church family and my Christ-loving gal-pals who stand with me, pray with me and inspire me.

I love the story in Exodus 17:8-13 about Joshua and the army of Israel fighting against the Amalekites, while Moses, Aaron, and Hur went up to the top of the mountain. As the battle rages below, Moses lifts his hands to God. When his hands are raised, Joshua and the Israelite army have the upper hand, but the Amalekites begin to win the battle when Moses lowers his hands. Eventually, Moses's arms grow weary, and he can't keep them raised any longer, so Aaron and Hur stand on either side and lift his hands until Joshua defeats the enemy. Every time I read this passage, tears flow. It is such a beautiful picture of the church, standing as one, with and for our brothers and sisters.

Sometimes in life, we can be battle-weary, barely able to keep a pinkie finger in the air, yet the fight is far from over. It's times like these that it's vital to be rooted in God's house with loving, godly people around us who can stand by our side and keep our hands raised until the battle is over. It's easy to choose to hide away, thinking, "People don't want or need to see me like this, so I'll stay away for a while." My advice – don't stay away from church! Even if you are hurting like crazy and it all feels so numb (that's exactly how Naomi was feeling) – keep going. I can testify to this from personal experience. It can take time, but God's house and his community of believers are where healing and restoration happen.

Who are Your Naomis?

As well as being a *Naomi* for others to follow after, it's imperative that we also recognise and honour the *Naomis* in our own lives. I know that I could not be the person I am today without some of the awe-inspiring women in my life. Women who I've looked up to, inspired me, challenged me and believed in me. Women who have shown me Jesus and how to live for Him through the seasons of life. Godly women, who choose righteousness, stand up for what's right and fight for justice in the face of adversity. These are the women who inspire me. They are brave, courageous, joyful, and passionate. They've walked hard roads, never losing faith or falling out of love with their Saviour, Jesus. Many of them are unaware of how they inspire me because they are not looking for glory or recognition. They are living out their lives for God and living them well.

It's essential to surround yourself with women like this. Women who can influence you for good and bring out the best in you, who pray and spend time in God's Word. Women who share similar values and morals. Women who praise and lift up rather than those who gossip and tear down.

There is also great value in surrounding yourself with women of all ages. We will naturally gravitate towards women of similar ages and those who are walking similar stages of life. Still, there is so much wealth in having friendships with older women. Take time to sit with these women and listen to their stories. They have lived through times that we know nothing about. They've seen revivals and miracles that we probably can't even fathom. They have seen the world change dramatically, and they have lived a life without mobile phones, the internet and all sorts of technology. Mind-blowing, right? Their stories are not just fascinating; they are full of so much depth and wisdom. There is a great deal we can learn from them. I genuinely believe we should never despise the elderly but should ALWAYS honour them. Their wisdom is priceless.

So when I chose the women I want to be around, women who can be *Naomis* in my life, there is one thing I'm looking for in these ladies. I want to be around beautiful women. However, I'm not just talking about surface-level beauty, rather a beauty that is founded in a loving relationship with the Father God. Beauty that comes from the stories of life that have shaped each one of them. We often look at the surface to define beauty. However, when I think about all the incredible women in my life, although they are all outwardly beautiful, what makes them exceedingly beautiful (and someone I admire and aspire to be like) is something you can't see with the human eye. Their beauty is in their character and attitude, how they love their family, how they face challenges and walk through life. It's even in how they approach their work and the day-to-day mundane routines in life. Remember that is what drew Ruth to Naomi. In Ruth's eyes, all those small, seemingly inconsequential things added up to something extraordinary.

Today women of God, let's rise up and rally together! Let's lead the way in being *'The Naomi Phenomenon'*, reaching out and leading our *Ruths* into their God-given destinies.

Chapter 8

Dealing With Disappointment

This chapter could potentially be the hardest to write. But, on the other hand, it might be the easiest because it is so personal and very close to home. It's about something I have had to journey through and am possibly still attempting to do. I also know it's not the last time I'll have to do this dance. In fact, it's something we have all faced head-on in our lifetime – DISAPPOINTMENT. I am pretty confident that there is not a single human being who hasn't been disappointed. Disappointment comes in all forms.

As a child, we experience disappointment when we lose a game, don't get the toy we wanted for Christmas, don't get picked for a team, don't get the teacher we were hoping for, and the list goes on. Disappointment can be over very small meaningless things, like that feeling you get when you bite into a peach that appeared to be completely perfect on the outside but was less than ordinary on the inside, or when you go to the store for ice cream, and they've sold out of your favourite flavour.

The Danger that Lurks

Now in my mind, disappointment is one of those 'meh' emotions. Meh' because it's not that big of a deal and perhaps not so clearly definable in comparison to other emotions. Not like other emotions that are easy to identify. There's no mistaking when someone is happy or full of deep sorrow. Anger is unmissable, and surprise or excitement is plain for all to see.

Disappointment though, well, it's not one of those emotions you can see, clearly written all over someone's face, and that is where the danger lies. Disappointment is a bit like Loki (huge apologies if you're not an Avengers fan). It's always lurking around under the surface, morphing into various forms and attaching itself to any emotional villain willing to play the part. Disappointment can sneak into our everyday lives without us even knowing it, and on its own, it's not such a bad thing.

However, sometimes life can throw us some huge disappointments. How we deal with these can make or break us because disappointment, if not dealt with, can attach itself to some pretty ugly things like anger, bitterness, unforgiveness, jealousy, and even hatred. Sadly, this can be to our detriment, leading to one's undoing. I believe the devil uses disappointment as one of his biggest weapons to steal people away from God.

The Day the Baby Died

There were two significant events in my life (not to say these have been the only instances) where I have had to battle with disappointment head-on. *'The day the baby died'* and *'The day the baby died'*. To say it is hard to write about these events is an understatement. I'm not writing for sympathy, but I promised myself in writing this book that I would be honest, true to myself, and write from my heart.

I feel to write about these seasons of disappointment because we all face them and it's how we walk through them that matters. I hope that in sharing about some of the dark times in my life, I can help and encourage others. Because, after the Winter comes the Spring. In the darkness, there is a light called hope, and dragging yourself through some of your worst days may very well lead to the birth of your finest hour.

I lost a baby.

It was my second pregnancy. I was exactly 12 weeks pregnant, and we had waited to tell everyone to make sure everything was okay. Finally, we had made it to the all-important 12-week mark. Today was the day, and it was going to be wonderful.

Except – it wasn't.

When I woke up that morning, I knew something wasn't quite right. The baby had possibly died about two weeks before, and I hadn't shown any signs until then. I felt numb and sad and angry and lost and, most of all, disappointed. I had to have a procedure to remove the baby, and when I awoke from the surgery, it was a feeling like I've never had or wish to have again. I was empty. A life that was growing inside me had died, and I was gutted. It's not uncommon to have a miscarriage. Many women do, but just because it is common doesn't mean that it is not significant. I hurt a great deal, and I struggled to let go of the disappointment and move forward.

I strongly believed that the baby was a girl, and we named her. That may seem odd to some, but for me, it helped with the grieving process. Time passes, and you heal from these things. God blessed us with a beautiful boy a year later, and I can't imagine life without my son. We named him Jethro, which means abundance, and he has brought an abundance of joy and love to our family. God is so good! He always brings healing to our brokenness and replaces our sorrow with joy. I've had visions during worship times of my little girl in Heaven with my grandmother, and she has told me that she is doing well, that Heaven is beautiful, and that Jesus is wonderful. We have talked with our children about the baby, and they know they have a sister waiting to meet them one day in Heaven.

When Disappointment Takes Hold

Grieving the loss of this baby was a difficult time for me, but what I didn't realise was that years later, I would experience another type of loss, a spiritual one. I referred to it earlier in this chapter as *'The day the baby died'* because the loss I felt during this time was just like that. However, looking back, it is also because this thing in my life was my baby.

I'm talking about my ministry.

I was holding onto it so tightly, and I'd let it become part of my identity. It wasn't the only thing in my life, but it was a big part of my life, and it had been for many years. It made me feel significant and validated, and when it was gone, I was lost.

That's when those niggling thoughts suddenly grew from tiny, little, insignificant weeds to big choking, strangling thorny bushes in my life. I was consumed by disappointment, pain, hurt, loss, and brokenness. I struggled to understand why for many, many months – years, if I'm honest. I grappled with things seeming so unfair. Life changed dramatically, which seemed to add to the anguish I was feeling.

As time passed and dragged into months and months, I began to feel guilt and shame towards myself. I thought I should be coping better, and I should be getting over these feelings. But the problem was I felt like I had no direction. I was moving on with life and getting involved in new things. However, for the first time in my life, I couldn't see an endpoint to all this pain. I couldn't find purpose or meaning in the things I was doing. More than ever before, I had to surrender myself entirely to God, trusting that He was carrying me. That He had it all worked out and that His plan for my life would become clear in due time.

The Choice to Trust in God

To be honest, these are the seasons when I've had to have more faith than ever because I haven't known or understood what God was doing in my life. Yes, walking through the valley of disappointment and waiting for the *'new baby to be born' (physically and spiritually)* have been the most challenging seasons of my life. But, when I look back over these times, a common thread enabled me to walk through them. It was the choice I made. A choice that only I could make to draw near to God. Even though I had no answers, even though I felt void of joy, even though everything felt completely unjust and unfair, I chose to keep putting myself in His presence. I had lots of people around me, loving on me, but deep down, I knew that this was an internal and personal journey of healing between God and me.

I could only feel whole again by putting myself in a place where God could hold me, love me and breathe His divine breath into me. How long did it take? Well, there is no time frame for these things, but if you continue choosing to put your disappointment into the loving arms of Jesus, instead of holding onto it, in time, you will find rest, wholeness, peace, joy, and a renewed purpose.

There's a beautiful story in the Bible of a woman who did just that. Her name was Hannah. I want to take some time delving into her story and how she exemplifies the way we as Christians should be dealing with disappointment. Before I begin, though, I'd like to share a poem I wrote telling her story, which is in 1Samuel 1 and 2:1-11.

PRELUDE TO HANNAH'S SONG

By Andrina Rijken

Wrestling
My soul is wrestling
A brooding, violent storm
A tempest rages
There is no rest from the torment within

Questions
Questions invade the peace that I long
Yet the answers remain out of reach
Far from my knowing
And so my longing grows

Faithful
Faithful is my life's theme
Yet all is futile
For all the goodness that surrounds
Does little to quench the longing

Taunting
Taunting words like arrows pierce
Mocked, misjudged, misunderstood
Despair overtakes
Disappointment makes a home

Empty
Empty and broken
"She is barren"
The words echo, and like a tornado
In violent ruin they destroy

Alone
Alone with You
The solace that I seek
No man can relinquish my suffering
But You…

…Almighty
Almighty my God, Father, King
I empty my heart to you
Hear my plea within this anguish
The one thing I ask

Mistaken
Mistaken by those looking in
Unoffended, no resistance, I will not flee
Steadfast I remain, unwavering
My honest vow is heard

Hope
Hope granted
Faith anticipates—a promise comes
I am strengthened
Though the time of fruition is unknown

Arriving
Arriving like the dawning of Spring
The promise prevails
Its beauty unrivalled
The earth breaks forth dancing in celebration

Returning
Returning to the place where you remembered me
I come, bringing fulfilment
Laid before you
May it be all you would it be

A seed
A seed speaks to the future
A barren generation hopeless and scorned
Journeys towards the break of day
A new promise in the waiting

HANNAH – Just a Little Bit of Her Backstory

Hannah's story is a beautiful narrative, depicting a regular Israelite family in need and the providence of God that moves in response to the plea of a broken woman. Its placement as the opening story to the book of Samuel is unusual when considering the greater narrative of Israel's history. However, in understanding the big picture of God's plan for Israel, this story is all the more powerful and pertinent.

If I may digress a moment to explain a little about the Old Testament and the background to this story. For some, this may seem unnecessary. However, I have learnt that it is incredibly powerful to understand where we have come from to deeply appreciate how far we have come through the immensely generous gift of God's love and salvation.

In our Protestant Bible, the book of Judges and Samuel are separated by the book of Ruth. However, the Hebrew Bible differs because Ruth does not sperate these two books. Instead, it is found in the latter portion of Israel's Scriptures known as the 'Writings'. This results in a chronological retelling of Israel's history from Joshua through Kings.

It is also important to understand that these books were originally written during the exile, specifically for the children of Israel who were banished in Babylon. The author intends to give an account of Israel's history, explaining how and why they ended up in exile.

Throughout the books of Joshua through Kings, the central theme is about God's covenant with Israel and the consequences that arise from both keeping and breaking covenant. You may be thinking, "That sounds like lots of rules to follow and God's damnation when His children don't." In my eyes, it's not quite like that. When I think about these books and God's covenant, I see a Father's love for His people, His willingness to show mercy time and time again, to do miracles, and work in power, to raise kings and prophets from obscurity in order to lead the nation of Israel. I see the outworking of His long-range plan, moving humankind closer and closer to salvation.

The story of Hannah begins as the era of the judges is coming to a close. This was a dark time in Israel's history and much like Hannah, Israel was spiritually barren. The closing verse of the book of Judges says:

In those days Israel had no king; everyone did as they saw fit (**Judges 21:25** **NIV**).

This period reminds me so much of the world we live in today. Everyone is going about their lives doing whatever they want, when they want and how they want. Throughout the book of Judges, Israel is on a cyclical spiral of demise. First, they sin and end up in peril. Then they repent and cry out to God. God powerfully intervenes and raises up a godly judge to deliver them, only for them to return to their former ways. This happens time and time again until the book closes on a very climactic note in the final verse – "There was no king...."

It reminds me of the olden days (I'm giggling under my breath about this), when you couldn't binge-watch your favourite TV series but had to wait 6-12 months before the next season came out to see what was going to happen next. Will he live or die? Is she really a Russian spy? Will they kiss, or are they destined to live without one another through infinite space and eternity (sigh)? I feel like Judges ends just like this. Will there be a king, or won't there? I'm sure the first readers of these books had the same question on their lips and couldn't wait to turn the page, anticipating a grand story about this great king. What a letdown it must have been to read:

There was a certain man from Ramathaim, a Zuphite from the hill country of Ephraim, whose name was Elkanah son of Jeroham, the son of Elihu, the son of Tohu, the son of Zuph, an Ephraimite. He had two wives; one was called Hannah and the other Peninnah. Peninnah had children, but Hannah had none
(1 Samuel 1:1-2 NIV).

Oh, but this is the genius of the author and the sign of a great literary work! Suddenly, shifting the focus onto new, seemingly menial characters who are so very pivotal. The way he leads the readers through intrigue to masterfully highlight God's breathtaking plan for His people and, in turn, all humankind. Suddenly the story comes alive, and the characters are all the more endearing as we relate to their plight and receive new layers of revelation from a story we have read many times before. It doesn't quite make sense, but the tension is palpable. God is on the move, and He's about to do something great. Let me break it down further.

Now Let's Get Down to Hannah

1 Samuel 1:1-8 explains the background for the remainder of the chapter, beginning by introducing Elkanah and summarising his origin and genealogy. Like any genealogy, it's not the most exciting read. However, genealogies are vital because they highlight that God is in the details. Who we are and where we have come from is significant to Him and our unfolding life story, even if it may seem mundane and boring. I'll come back to this again later in the story, but God wants to be completely involved in our lives and wants us to give Him every part, even the mundane and boring.

The next thing we learn about Elkanah in verse 2 is he had two wives, and one was barren. Given the order of the names in this verse, Hannah followed by Peninnah, we can conclude that Hannah was Elkanah's first wife.[4] The fact that polygamy (although in accordance with the culture of the ancient world[5]) was not the Biblical norm, especially amongst commoners, suggests Elkanah took a second wife because Hannah was infertile and could not provide an heir.[6] "Barrenness in ancient times was the ultimate tragedy for a married woman,"[7] which further added to Hannah's plight. In the whole scheme of this family, Hannah was

---

[4] Stephen B. Chapman, *1 Samuel as Christian Scripture*: A Theological Commentary, (Grand Rapids, Michigan: William B. Eerdmans Publishing, 2016), 64.

[5] Ronald F. Youngblood, Tremper Longman III, and David E. Garland, *1 and 2 Samuel*: The Expositor's Bible Commentary, (Grand Rapids, Michigan: Harper Collins Christian Publishing, 2017), 54c.

[6] Stephen J. Andrews, Robert D. Bergen, and Max Anders, *1, 2 Samuel*: Holman Old Testament Commentary, (Nashville, Tennessee: B&H Publishing Group, 2009), 23.

[7] Youngblood, Longman and Garland, 54d.

nothing more than a trophy wife. Without being able to give birth to an heir, she could contribute nothing.

Disappointment can make us feel much like Hannah did – useless. It can put us in a stalemate where we feel stuck. As the story progresses, we will see that although Hannah had nothing to offer according to her culture's standards, she knew where to take her disappointment. She didn't try to fake it, as many of us often do, pretending everything is ok.

Sometimes when we are going through a challenge or dealing with disappointment, we think being positive and declaring victory despite our circumstances is the Christian thing to do. We wrongfully perceive that we can't let the world see our pain. Yet often, we are doing this in our own strength instead of allowing God's grace to help us pass through the valley. Hannah didn't hide her pain and disappointment from her family, but she did find solace in the House of God, and there she presented her lament as a beautiful act of worship.

It is Actually Okay to Lament

We should never underestimate the power of pouring out our laments to God. There is a misconception that worship must always be uplifting and full of victory and faith, which I believe is true in the corporate sense. However, in the Bible, the majority of Psalms were laments. I think there is something so beautiful in bringing our laments to God.

Earlier I said God wants every part of our lives. Well, this is true of our disappointments as well. God doesn't just want to share in your finest moments of life. No, He wants all of you, the brave and the broken. Think about the people you are closest to in your life. Do they see all of you or only the good bits? Do you share everything with them or only your highlight reel? My husband and children have seen it all. They've seen me love, hate, regret, cry, shout for joy, and be bitterly disappointed. If I'm made in the image of God, then how I relate to my closest loved ones is a model for how I act with God. It means He doesn't just get my highlight reel. He gets it all: my highs, my lows, my joy, and my sadness. That day in the house of God, Hannah brought her all.

But I've Checked All the Boxes!

The third detail about Elkanah and his family was they were devoutly religious. Verse 3 describes how Elkanah and his family travelled to Shiloh year after year to worship and offer sacrifices to the Lord.[8] As the story unfolds, we learn that despite the family's faithfulness to worship the Lord, Hannah remains without a child. As a result, their yearly pilgrimage to Shiloh only heightened her anguish.

This situation is something that I have never been able to reason with my own mind. Why do bad things happen to good people? Even more so, why do bad things happen to godly people who have always followed in God's ways and given their lives to serve Him with all their hearts? I've had this conversation with God many times, especially when considering disappointments I've had to face. "I don't understand God. Why is this happening to me? I've always done the right thing. I've lived a godly life, I've kept your commandments, I've never rebelled or strayed from you. So why am I suffering? Shouldn't I be living a victorious, blessed life?"

Hannah was no different. She and her family were following the religious traditions of her culture to the letter. They were doing all the right things. How demoralising it must have felt to still not have the one thing she desired. Yet, she doesn't try to use self-righteousness as a bargaining chip to justify why she should get her way, as we so often do. What does she do instead? She humbly brings her supplication to God.

---

[8] Andrews, Bergen and Anders, 24.

ANDRINA E. RIJKEN

1 Samuel 1:10-11 (NIV)

In her deep anguish Hannah prayed to the Lord, weeping bitterly. And she made a vow, saying, "Lord Almighty, if you will only look on your servant's misery and remember me, and not forget your servant but give her a son, then I will give him to the Lord for all the days of his life, and no razor will ever be used on his head."

The Seed I've Received I Will Sow

Notice how simple her prayer is. She doesn't try and lace it with her own piousness and qualifications or bargain with God. She asks for what she desires. Then she does something extraordinary. She makes a vow. However, this vow is unlike vows typically made in ancient times, which were a quid pro quo type of arrangement. Instead, Hannah vows to bring an offering before God if He answers her prayer. She vows to sow her son as a seed into God's House. Her vow is an act of faith that speaks to the future about who Samuel will be. Hannah vows to give him back to God as a seed that will in turn bless all of Israel. How completely selfless! Her plan is not to keep her son for herself, which would be perfectly appropriate for any loving mother. No, she realises that when God blesses us, it is not for ourselves. Instead, it should flow through us so that those around us (in this case, an entire nation) may also benefit from the blessings God has given us.

I'm reminded of a worship song by Hillsong Worship titled, *The Desert Song*, which speaks about praising God even in dry and challenging seasons. The lyrics of the final verse say:

*"This is my prayer in the harvest
When favour and providence flow*

I know I'm filled to be emptied again
The seed I've received I will sow"[9]

Hannah's story is so beautiful because out of her humble lament before God, she births something much greater than herself – a child who would lead Israel into the era of kingship. Out of nothingness, God birthed greatness. God isn't bad, and he cannot cause bad things to happen to us, but He will give us the grace to walk through them. If we keep our hearts soft the way Hannah did, then disappointment won't win the fight. We won't come out the other side dilapidated and maimed. No, we will come out rejoicing and singing into the future, just as Hannah did when she sang in *1Samuel 2:1-10*.

So don't despise your disappointments. Instead, take them to God. Allow Him to refine you in the fire. In doing this, you position yourself to receive the wondrous things He has in store for your future and the future of those for generations to come.

Oh Man! There's Always People!!!

Before moving on from the story of Hannah, we need to consider the other characters in this narrative. Disappointment is rarely an isolated event that happens internally. Usually, there are people involved. Whether it is a person who causes the disappointment or a person who tries to add their two cents worth along the way, there are always people involved. Unfortunately, more often than not, even if they are well-meaning and trying to be supportive, they tend to just make matters worse. Don't get me wrong; God will bring people into our lives who will be wonderfully supportive and help us journey through disappointment. However, the truth of the matter is, that usually there are people involved who seem

---

[9] Brooke Ligertwood, Hillsong Worship, "Desert Song," recorded 9 March 2008, track 3 on *This is Our God*, Hillsong Publishing, 2007, compact disc.

to stir the pot, which can make dealing with our disappointment even harder.

In Hannah's case, this was no different. In addition to her already dire circumstances, there were three people who exacerbated Hannah's suffering by being particularly insensitive and unsympathetic. Yet she responds so graciously, again showing us how we as Christians should respond towards people during these challenging times in our lives.

The Mean Girl

The first person is Peninnah, the other wife or, as I like to call her, 'The Mean Girl'. We can all probably recall that person when we were in high school. Not necessarily a girl, but someone who was just plain mean. Possibly even a bully. This was Peninnah. There was no camaraderie between Hannah and Peninnah. Hannah was Peninnah's nemesis, her rival, and to that end, Peninnah taunted Hannah. She knew Elkanah loved Hannah more, so she used her ability to bear children to put Hannah in her place. "You might be loved, but you are nothing in the eyes of society!"

The Insensitive Husband

Then there's Elkanah, Hannah's husband. Poor guy! Did he have a bad case of putting his foot in his mouth! He couldn't empathise with Hannah at all, so he said the first stupid thing that popped into his head:

> *1 Samuel 1:8 (NIV)*
>
> *Her husband Elkanah would say to her, "Hannah, why are you weeping? Why don't you eat? Why are you downhearted? Don't I mean more to you than ten sons?"*

Talk about utterly insensitive!

So, she is despised and bullied by Peninnah and entirely misunderstood by her husband. Despite having grounds to retaliate and give them both what for, Hannah demonstrates how to respond in the face of adversity. She shuts out the external pressures of society's expectations and opens herself up to the presence of God.

The Undiscerning Man of God

It doesn't end there, though, because Hannah is about to encounter one more person who could make or break this entire story. Eli, the undiscerning priest, who accuses her of being drunk! She's pouring out her heart to God, pleading with God to intervene, and Eli thinks she's drunk.

Well, I never (says I, totally tongue in cheek)! Have you ever heard such a thing? A man of God who didn't get it quite right? I do feel sorry for Eli. He has completely misread this scenario. Chalk it up to having enough problems to deal with in his own family. He's just not having a good day. But believe it or not, just like regular people, ministers have bad days too, and they don't always get it right. If Peninnah's taunting and Elkanah's insensitivity weren't enough to send Hannah over the edge, surely Eli's judgmental attitude and false accusations give her the right to take offence and storm out of the House of God.

And there it is – OFFENCE.

Meaning – disappointment morphing into something and rearing its ugly head as indignation and offence. I've seen all too many taken out by the power of offence. Not Hannah though, she responds with such grace and humility. She doesn't challenge or berate Eli, nor does she question his qualifications as the so-called man of God. Instead, she simply clarifies the situation:

1 Samuel 1:12-16 (NIV)

As she kept on praying to the Lord, Eli observed her mouth. Hannah was praying in her heart, and her lips were moving but her voice was not heard. Eli thought she was drunk and said to her, "How long are you going to stay drunk? Put away your wine." "Not so, my lord," Hannah replied, "I am a woman who is deeply troubled. I have not been drinking wine or beer; I was pouring out my soul to the Lord. Do not take your servant for a wicked woman; I have been praying here out of my great anguish and grief."

Position Yourself in His Presence

I marvel at her composure! How is it that a woman who has endured so much pain, does not take offence? The answer is simple because she had been in the presence of God. She had been worshipping Him.

That, I believe, is the key to walking through disappointment – WORSHIP. Worship is never about how we feel. It is always about God and how wonderful He is. He doesn't stipulate that we must be all put together to worship Him. He says, "Just come." Pour out your heart, whether it's pouring out joy to Him or immense sorrow – come. When Eli understands that this is Hannah's position, He blesses her, saying, *"Go in peace, be whole, nothing missing broken or lacking."* Hannah's prayer is not answered immediately but she is able to rest in the comfort that God has heard her heart's cry.

It is easy to become offended when disappointment strikes – offended at family, friends, the church, the pastor, another brother or sister in Christ, even at God. We run from the House of God when the House is where we should be. Hannah positioned herself for a miracle by drawing near to God in worship. It wasn't necessarily pretty, but it was pure.

In my own life, worship and being in God's House has carried me through my darkest times. Rather than tell everybody I knew about my disappointments, I've spent time worshipping, both privately and corporately and many times in tears, bucket loads of tears. God has always come through for me!

Sometimes it's a process and journeying through disappointment takes time. It can strike unexpectedly. You can be travelling just fine along your merry way, and out of nowhere, it pops up, and you feel like you're back to square one. That's why you have to constantly draw near to God and never stop worshipping Him. No matter how I feel, I always know God is worthy, and even if no one around seems to understand, just as He did for Hannah, He will understand the purity of my worship.

Have people said stupid things to me? YES!! Have I been offended? My word – YES!! Have I always had answers and been able to rationalise things – definitely, NO!! But I've always kept coming to God, because away from Him, I will always be broken. It's only in Him that I can be whole and free from disappointment.

The story of Hannah reminds us to remain steadfast and run to God rather than people. As we give our broken and seemingly insignificant lives over to God, hope stirs and gives way to faith. Faith gives birth to the promise, and the promise reveals a vision for the future – a future not only for ourselves but also for the generations to follow. This is paramount. Our future is always worth fighting for. Disappointments, they will come and go. Therefore, our desire should not only be that God will change the impossible situations in our immediate lives, but that these changes will affect change for our future and the future of those around us.

Chapter 9

Laughing At the Future Part 1: Delighting in His Word

I previously mentioned what a wonderful husband I have. I am tremendously blessed to be married to him, and I can't thank God enough for him. He really is a one in a billion guy. I know I have also raved about what a funny guy he is, but if you'll humour me a little longer (sorry, that was a bad pun – I can see my husband and children shaking their heads at how unfunny that was). My husband always uses puns (his are actually good, unlike mine) and plays on words to draw out a little smirk or giggle from those around. I always have to be on my toes because he is so quick-witted. I don't always get his jokes straight away. I love this about my husband because there is never a dull moment in our life, and in the last 20 plus years that I have known him, there's not a day that has gone by that he hasn't made me laugh. He is exactly the right person for me. As I have said (probably multiple times now),

I can be so serious and intense, and my husband always knows how to lighten things up.

The world we live in today is super intense, and it is so easy to get caught up in its tornado of despair. We need to lighten up. As we come towards the close of this book, I believe God is saying,

> *"Laugh at the future! Walk into your future laughing. Be filled with great joy, knowing that I, your Father God, will do all that you dream of and more. Don't be afraid to laugh at the impossibilities and the things that are yet to come to pass because great joy is coming to those who will wait for my timing and never stop believing."*

Cultivate Joy

Have you ever heard someone say, "I'll be happy when……. …I meet my dream guy, I get married, I have a baby, I get the house of my dreams, I get to travel all over the world?" Maybe you've said these things yourself. The thing about happiness, though, is that it is circumstantial and dictated by external influences. This means it is temporary and not lasting. It comes and goes and has little substance. I'm happy when I have my morning coffee, and I feel happy when I see a picture of a Golden Retriever puppy, but then my child sticks his face in mine and demands me to make him breakfast, and the moment's over. I joke, but happiness is very much like this.

Joy, on the other hand, is lasting and comes from within. Joy is an emotion that can weather the storm and still cause us to smile and laugh even when our external circumstances try to dictate otherwise. Joy is what we need to cultivate in our hearts. We can't buy it by filling our lives with material things, experiences, or even our relationships. Joy is precious and should be treasured because it is a gift from God. We need to consciously choose joy every day and be deliberate about allowing it to flow from us regardless of our circumstances. God wants us to be dispersers of joy to those around us. In a world full of people seeking ultimate happiness, He wants us to be the point of difference, carriers of joy to those who are yet to encounter the wonder of His life-giving joy.

So How Do We Cultivate Joy?

You might, be reading this and thinking, "Great advice, but I don't feel joyful at all, let alone happy. How am I supposed to be joyful despite my circumstances? I can barely make it from day to day. The very thought of cultivating joy sounds sheer exhausting." I can relate to those feelings. Sometimes it is difficult to be joyful, and it can be hard work.

Now, the advice I'm about to give you might be some of the best advice you'll ever get in your whole life. Big call, I know, but before I give it to you, I'm going to warn you that it might not be the type of advice you want to hear…

Let me digress a moment. When I was growing up, and I had a problem, from something as simple as a headache to a big exam or issues with my friends or a decision I had to make, I would always go to my Mum for advice. I don't think there is a single time I can remember that she didn't start her response with, "Just pray in tongues." And every time, I would roll my eyes and say, "Oh, Mum, please!!!"

…Well, the advice I'm about to give is very similar, and you may roll your eyes, but since I can't see you, I'll forgive you. So just hear me out…

Go to the Word!

If you need a good dose of joy in your life, GO TO THE WORD. Start by confessing and speaking aloud scriptures about joy. Then begin to search the Word for more verses that will re-energise your soul. That's what I love so much about the Word. It is full of hidden treasures, and there is always something new to discover. For example, the Bible talks quite a lot about laughter and joy. Have a look at these fantastic scriptures:

> ***Job 8:21 (NLT):*** *He will once again fill your mouth with laughter and your lips with shouts of joy.*
>
> ***Psalm 30:11 (NLT):*** *You have turned my mourning into joyful dancing. You have taken away my clothes of mourning and clothed me with joy.*
>
> ***Psalm 65:12-13 (NLT):*** *The grasslands of the wilderness become a lush pasture, and the hillsides blossom with joy. The meadows are clothed with flocks of sheep, and the valleys are carpeted with grain. They all shout and sing for joy!*
>
> ***Psalm 96:12 (NLT):*** *Let the fields and their crops burst out with joy! Let the trees of the forest sing for joy.*
>
> ***Psalm 98:4 (NLT):*** *Shout to the Lord, all the earth; break out in praise and sing for joy!*
>
> ***Psalm 126:2 (NLT):*** *We were filled with laughter, and we sang for joy. And the other nations said, "What amazing things the Lord has done for them."*
>
> ***Proverbs 17:22 (NLT):*** *A cheerful heart is good medicine, but a broken spirit saps a person's strength.*
>
> ***Proverbs 31:25 (NLT):*** *She is clothed with strength and dignity, and she laughs without fear of the future.*

Isaiah 55:12 (NLT): *You will live in joy and peace. The mountains and hills will burst into song, and the trees of the field will clap their hands!*

Jeremiah 31:13 (NLT): *The young women will dance for joy, and the men – old and young – will join in the celebration. I will turn their mourning into joy. I will comfort them and exchange their sorrow for rejoicing.*

John 15:11 (NLT): *I have told you these things so that you will be filled with my joy. Yes, your joy will overflow!*

1 Peter 1:8 (NLT): *You love him even though you have never seen him. Though you do not see him now, you trust him; and you rejoice with a glorious, inexpressible joy.*

Why is the Word of God so Important for Cultivating Joy?

I started this book by talking about Psalm 1, and as I draw towards the end of this book, it's an opportune time to look a little more deeply at this Psalm:

PSALM 1:1-6 (NIV)

1 Blessed is the one who does not walk in step with the wicked or stand in the way that sinners take or sit in the company of mockers,

2 but whose delight is in the law of the Lord, and who meditates on his law day and night.

3 That person is like a tree planted by streams of water, which yields its fruit in season and whose leaf does not wither – whatever they do prospers.

4 Not so the wicked! They are like chaff that the wind blows away.

5 Therefore the wicked will not stand in the judgment, nor sinners in the assembly of the righteous.

6 For the Lord watches over the way of the righteous, but the way of the wicked leads to destruction.

The Book of Psalms opens with a short yet beautiful work of poetry that offers humankind the choice of two paths. In literary terms, it acts as the prologue, introducing the reader to what the rest of the book will be about. It's an invitation from the author to the reader:

"Will you come with me and follow the path of the righteous, journeying in discovery and wonderment at all of the blessings of Father God? Or will you take another path, turning from the wonders of my truth, leading towards the path of destruction?"

The outcome is clearly laid out for the reader. Blessing? Destruction? Delight in my Word, and you will know blessing. Follow the wicked, and you will only know destruction and death.

Psalm 1 is full of parallels, metaphors, and symbolism that echo the story of Eden. For those who delight in the Law of the Lord, they will be like a tree planted by streams of water. This is symbolic of the Tree of Life in the Garden of Eden. The Word of God is our lifeblood, and without it, we cannot grow. Conversely, the wicked are likened to *'chaff'* or dust, which again links back to the garden and the creation of man. *'From dust we came, and to dust we return.'*

Yet again, the message of this Psalm is clear. God's Word is our lifeblood. If we don't choose to become lovers of His Word, then metaphorically, we are nothing more than dust. This is the essence of this Psalm. What path will you choose? To love His Word and thrive or turn away and be like chaff blown about by the torrent of life?

I can't imagine when it's laid out so plainly that many of us would choose the latter. But come tomorrow, when life gets in the way (oh, and it sure is good at doing so!), that choice becomes a little harder to make.

So I'm here to encourage you because I'm not perfect either. There have been times when I have neglected the Word of God and haven't given it first place in my life as I should. So, be a lover of the Word. Just start. Start reading your Bible like you never have before and determine to fall in love with the Word of God. Choose to join with the writer of Psalm 1 and enter the journey. Traverse the pages and begin to anticipate excitement, revelation, and you guessed it, JOY!

If you're struggling to cultivate joy, then look no further. The Word of God is full of scriptures to encourage and uplift. Here are some of my favourite Bible verses that I turn to regularly for encouragement and inspiration:

Jeremiah 6:16 (NIV)

This is what the Lord says: "Stand at the crossroads and look; ask for the ancient paths, ask where the good way is, and walk in it, and you will find rest for your souls".

Habakkuk 3:18-19 (NLT)

Yet I will rejoice in the Lord! I will be joyful in the God of my salvation! The Sovereign Lord is my strength! He makes me as surefooted as a deer, able to tread upon the heights.

Isaiah 41:10 (NLT)

Don't be afraid, for I am with you. Don't be discouraged, for I am your God. I will strengthen you and help you. I will hold you up with my victorious right hand.

Isaiah 46:4 (NIV)

Even to your old age and grey hairs I am he, I am he who will sustain you. I have made you and I will carry you; I will sustain you and I will rescue you.

Isaiah 49:15-16 (NIV)

Can a mother forget the baby at her breast and have no compassion on the child she has borne? Though she may forget, I will not forget you! See, I have engraved you on the palms of my hands; your walls are ever before me.

Ephesians 3:16-20 (TPT)

And I pray that he would unveil within you the unlimited riches of his glory and favour until supernatural strength floods your innermost being with his divine might and explosive power. Then, by constantly using your faith, the life of Christ will be released deep inside you, and the resting place of his love will become the very source and root of your life. Then you will be empowered to discover what every holy one experiences – the great magnitude of the astonishing love of Christ in all its dimensions. How deeply intimate and far-reaching is his love! How enduring and inclusive it is! Endless love beyond measurement that transcends our understanding – this extravagant love pours into you until you are filled to overflowing with the fullness of God! Never doubt God's mighty power to work in you and accomplish all this. He will achieve infinitely more than your greatest request, your most unbelievable dream, and exceed your wildest imagination! He will outdo them all, for his miraculous power constantly energises you.

Romans 8:38-39 (TPT)

So *now I live with the confidence that there is nothing in the universe with the power to separate us from God's love. I'm convinced that his love will triumph over death, life's troubles, fallen angels, or dark rulers in the Heavens. There is nothing in our present or future circumstances that can weaken his love. There is no power above us or beneath us – no power that could ever be found in the universe that can distance us from God's passionate love, which is lavished upon us through our Lord Jesus, the Anointed One!*

Ephesians 2:10 (TPT)

We have become his poetry, a re-created people that will fulfil the destiny he has given each of us, for we are joined to Jesus, the Anointed One. Even before we were born, God planned in advance our destiny and the good works we would do to fulfil it!

I have already shared one poem in this book. I guess writing poetry from time to time is something I like to do. So, if you don't mind, I'd like to share another poem I wrote about the special relationship I have had with the Bible throughout my life. I hope in sharing this that you might consider what the Word of God means to you. That it might cause you to reflect on the paths that the Word of God has travelled with you, or perhaps, you have travelled with it. May these words remind you never to let go of your love for His Word. To always be expectant that you can find joy within its pages. Perhaps, just as the Psalmist did, I am inviting you to take the Father's hand and take part in the dance of a lifetime with Him.

THE SCARLET THREAD

by Andrina Rijken

I remember when
Just a little girl
I found a scarlet thread
I saw it weave and wind its way
Around a many tree
It seemed to beckon in a whisper
Calling out to me

So grasping hold
I took the thread
And followed down its path
There was no rhyme or reason then
But a journey tugging on my heart
Yet to behold the final tapestry
I was only at the start

The thread led me
To an ancient book
Penned by scribes of old
As I turned each page in wonder
I heard the echo of a voice
The kind words of a Father saying

ANDRINA E. RIJKEN

"Child you have a choice"

The thread led me on
Between the pages
Twisting and twirling along the way
As I traversed the valleys and the mountains
Every page revealed His face
A beauty unimagined
The story of love and grace

Some would say
The stories of the Old
Do not belong with the New
But the thread led me to discover
That all was intertwined
The beginning from the ending
Had only one thing in mind

And just like that
In a blink of an eye
The girl became a woman
She stood before a mirror
Holding thread in hand
A life she'd lived discovering
The Master's divine plan

And though she now
A woman grown
The thread she still holds tightly
And knowing she is still becoming
Onward the thread it draws her

Everyday the pages hold new discovery
His words how they consume her

And in the quiet
When all is still
She utters thanks to her Saviour
For in following the twists and turns
She revels in truth so profound
For etched within the scarlet thread
Her very name she found

You see the scarlet thread
Is the Saviour's love
The ancient book, His Word
The girl is me and this my journey
Of following the King
To grasp the thread my greatest choice
Of this one thing I sing!

Chapter 10

Laughing At the Future Part 2: Today's Laughter Is Tomorrow's Joy

Joy is more than just a mere emotion. God-given joy is a force to be reckoned with. As we dive deeper and deeper into God's Word, the joy found in the revelation of His Word and promises begins to grow, and it can't be contained. We have to learn to allow the joy within us to spring forth and fulfil its prophetic purpose every day of our lives. In the mundane and the magnificent. Through the challenges and the triumphs. When we don't understand and in the certainty of walking out our God-given destiny.

There is a woman in the Bible who did just that. In skimming over her story, it's easy to mistake this woman for one who seemed to have little faith, but God saw otherwise. When we read her story through our natural, human senses, we're quick to see a woman with many flaws. I love that my Father God, and Saviour always looks through eyes of love and grace and sees something so much more. The more I meditate on this story, the more I see God's hand of grace at work in every aspect of this narrative. Grace is such a wonderful gift. We are so undeserving of God's love and devotion, but He gives it anyway. Even with all our junk and baggage, God doesn't give a second thought to granting us favour. It is so crazy you can't help but laugh at his unfathomable gift. As we delve into this story let's look with eyes of grace and uncover the powerful truth of how the matriarch of our faith gave joy to the world.

Sarah's Story

It all starts way back in the book of Genesis, with a pretty little lady named Sarah. I know she was pretty, stunning actually because twice in Genesis, it tells how she caught the eye of Pharaoh and later King Abimelek and was taken into their palaces. I could go off on a tangent about how silly Abraham was to allow that to happen, not just once, but twice. However, that's a discussion for another time…

Despite Sarah's outward beauty, like Hannah, she was barren. However, she was not only barren. The Bible says she was past the age of being able to bear children. In other words, she was post-menopausal. So, biologically, it was not humanly possible for her to conceive or carry a child. And this is where we take up the story in Genesis 18. Abraham had been given two phenomenal promises in Genesis 12 and 15, where God declares his descendants would outnumber the stars in the sky and the grains of sand on the shore. God had also given Abraham and Sarah new names, and now they were about to have an unprecedented face-to-face encounter with God himself and two angelic messengers.

ANDRINA E. RIJKEN

Genesis 18:1-15 (NLT)

The Lord appeared again to Abraham near the oak grove belonging to Mamre. One day Abraham was sitting at the entrance to his tent during the hottest part of the day. He looked up and noticed three men standing nearby. When he saw them, he ran to meet them and welcomed them, bowing low to the ground. "My lord," he said, "if it pleases you, stop here for a while. Rest in the shade of this tree while water is brought to wash your feet. And since you've honoured your servant with this visit, let me prepare some food to refresh you before you continue on your journey." "All right," they said. "Do as you have said." So Abraham ran back to the tent and said to Sarah, "Hurry! Get three large measures of your best flour, knead it into dough, and bake some bread." Then Abraham ran out to the herd and chose a tender calf and gave it to his servant, who quickly prepared it. When the food was ready, Abraham took some yogurt and milk and the roasted meat, and he served it to the men. As they ate, Abraham waited on them in the shade of the trees. "Where is Sarah, your wife?" the visitors asked. "She's inside the tent," Abraham replied. Then one of them said, "I will return to you about this time next year, and your wife, Sarah, will have a son!" Sarah was listening to this conversation from the tent. Abraham and Sarah were both very old by this time, and Sarah was long past the age of having children. So she laughed silently to herself and said, "How could a worn-out woman like me enjoy such pleasure, especially when my master – my husband – is also so old?" Then the Lord said to Abraham, "Why did Sarah laugh? Why did she say, 'Can an old woman like me have a baby?' Is anything too hard for the Lord? I will return about this time next year, and Sarah will have a son." Sarah was afraid, so she denied it, saying, "I didn't laugh." But the Lord said, "No, you did laugh."

When God Comes on the Scene

This is some story! Let's start with the fact that when the three messengers arrived, Abraham mistook them for mere men. God, who Abraham had encountered before and made a covenant promise with Him, came in physical form. Yet, at first, Abraham didn't recognise Him! I would love to profess I am constantly at one with the Lord and am ever aware of His presence, but like Abraham, there are probably times when God shows up in my life, and I don't immediately recognise Him. How many times has the Holy Spirit gone ahead and worked to line things up for me, and it's not till after the fact that hindsight kicks in. I'm like, "Ooohhh, now I see it. That was a God thing!" I think if this were a scene from NCIS, then Gibbs would be smacking Abraham over the back of his head, and rightly so! Yet our God is so loving. He just kept gently prodding Abraham until he finally got on the same page.

The narrative points out that it was the hottest part of the day, and Abraham was resting by his tent. I love that! Even though it was hot, Abraham could rest, and that's when God showed up. Right in the middle of the heat. Hallelujah!! When life turns up the heat, we can rest assured that God will show up and bring deliverance! Woohoo!! (Insert Happy Dance!)

On seeing who he thinks are travellers, Abraham responds as expected in the ancient culture by washing their feet and refreshing them with water. Suddenly his eyes are opened to who these men are, and he recognises that they are more than just mere men. He goes above and beyond what is expected in the ancient culture, urging Sarah and the servants to prepare a feast, which he then serves to his visitors.

I would be remiss if I didn't acknowledge what a beautiful picture of worship this is. Sometimes we tiptoe into the presence of God, not quite sure of our place. We offer up the little sacrifice of praise that we have, and as we linger before our God, our eyes become open to the magnificence of who God is. Our praise swells and becomes a magnanimous feast, our only desire, to minister unto our merciful, loving God. I believe this was the heart of Abraham that day. God had already done so much for him, made a covenant promise, given him a new name. Now he had come to visit Abraham personally. There was no more appropriate response than to minister before his LORD. Oh, that we would have eyes to see our LORD when He is present and never miss an opportunity to minister at His feet.

He Sees Us Even When We Feel Unseen

Interestingly, Sarah is behind the scenes as these events transpire, yet she does not go unnoticed. In Ancient Near Eastern culture, women were not present in the company of male visitors. So, the fact that the LORD knew not only of her presence, but also her name was confounding. It further confirmed that the LORD himself was present in their midst.

It can be so easy when we go through the daily grind, doing things that don't seem to have much impact to think what we do is inconsequential, and God is not present in these menial types of activities. We talk about God being with us through the highs and lows, but He's there through the completely normal (possibly boring), ordinary stuff too. Our Father God wants to be a part of everything in our lives, not just the two ends of the spectrum. He wants to be there for us when we are rejoicing and also in the depths of our despair. He sees our everyday efforts, and they are of equal importance to Him.

You may feel your gifts and talents are unseen and unused by man, but God sees you, and He knows your heart. He has a divine purpose for you that no one else can fulfil. We need to learn to rest in that. It's easy to get uptight when things are not happening. It's hard to be patient. Remember, only you can fulfil the purpose you were born for – no one else. So if you think you have been overlooked or it's taking a long time for your opportunity to come, rest in the assurance that it is coming and it will come at the perfect appointed time. Don't sweat the small stuff. Keep doing what you're doing. The Father sees you, and He is setting out the path before you. The way that only you can walk out in this life.

Did She Just Laugh at God??!!

Keeping with cultural tradition, the LORD addresses Abraham with a message for Sarah, prophesying she would give birth to a son named Isaac within the year. This is where the story takes an interesting turn. Let's take another look:

Genesis 18:12-15 (NLT)

So she laughed silently to herself and said, "How could a worn-out woman like me enjoy such pleasure, especially when my master – my husband – is also so old?" Then the Lord said to Abraham, "Why did Sarah laugh? Why did she say, 'Can an old woman like me have a baby?' Is anything too hard for the Lord? I will return about this time next year, and Sarah will have a son." Sarah was afraid, so she denied it, saying, "I didn't laugh." But the Lord said, "No, you did laugh."

Sarah had the audacity to laugh at the promise of God. Not only that, but when God Himself asks her why she laughed, she lies to him and denies it. Talk about a major faux pas! She puts her foot in it by laughing and then makes matters worse by lying! AWKWARD! You have to love these awkward moments in the Bible. Let's linger here for a moment and ponder all these things.

There's Power in a Name

It can be so easy to overlook the significance of God changing not only Abraham's name but also Sarah's. God was completely turning patriarchal society on its head by doing this. He was making a statement to Abraham and to the generations to come, saying, "Through both Abraham and Sarah shall I fulfil my covenant promise." God was letting Sarah know that she had a place in His plan right alongside her husband. What an incredible picture of God liberating and empowering women to live out their true purpose!

Through Jesus' death and resurrection, God has done the same to every single born again believer. He has given us a new name. We are no longer children of darkness, but we are sons and daughters of the King of Kings. God has liberated and empowered us. Just like Sarah, we need to rise up and be all that our new name declares us to be.

Romans 8:15-17 (TPT)

But you have received the "Spirit of full acceptance," enfolding you into the family of God. And you will never feel orphaned, for as he rises up within us, our spirits join him in saying the words of tender affection, "Beloved Father!" For the Holy Spirit makes God's fatherhood real to us as he whispers into our innermost being, "You are God's beloved child!" And since we are his true children, we qualify to share all his treasures, for indeed, we are heirs of God himself.

I love the new name God gave to her, Sarah, meaning *'princess'*. I smile at this because it has a father's love for his daughter written all over it. Sarah was God's pride and joy, the apple of His eye, His princess. It paints a beautiful picture of how God sees us when we come to

Him. Through Jesus, we are His sons and daughters, His princes and princesses, His pride and joy, the apple of His eye and He has nothing but love and adoration for us. I can't help but smile at this thought! As we read on in this story, we will see how God's father heart for Sarah, His princess, is evident.

I am wonderfully blessed because I have a very special relationship with my Father. I have no doubt that he sees me as his little princess even though I am a grown woman. I still relish his hugs and want to know that he approves of me, and I make him proud. While my Dad has always cherished me like his princess, he has also empowered me to be strong, have dreams and goals, go for them, and never give up. It is true in this story also. In calling Sarah His princess, God was not only declaring she was a daughter of the King but that she was also a warrior and an unstoppable force in the kingdom of God. When God calls us into His kingdom, it is no different. He cherishes us as His children and also empowers us to be formidable warriors in His kingdom.

Grace Undeserved

Perhaps one of the reasons Sarah laughed was because she couldn't see herself this way. She was having a hard time accepting God's grace for herself. Sometimes it's easier to accept God showering grace down on others, but when it is our turn, we immediately disqualify ourselves by coming up with all the reasons why we don't deserve it. Sarah did just that. What she saw in the natural hindered her from seeing who she truly was in God's eyes and what was possible in the supernatural.

The idea of her giving birth to a child at her age was insane! There was no way she could get her head around it. But it would take an encounter with the Most High God. An encounter of unmerited, undeserved grace to cause Sarah to open up to the possibility that God could lift the limitations on her life and use her for something great.

If you are waiting for all your ducks to line up in the natural before you jump in, you're going to be waiting a very long time. So God wants you to stop trying to make everything perfect and start allowing Him to wrap His blanket of grace around you. It is in His grace that we are made perfect. It is in His grace that we find hope to smile and laugh at the promises that are still to come.

There is a song I love by Mercy Me titled *'Grace Got You'*. The lyrics to this song beautifully express the joy that is found when we immerse ourselves in grace. The chorus goes like this:

> "Sing so the back row hears you
> Glide 'cause walking just won't do
> Dance, you don't have to know how to
> Ever since, ever since grace got you
> Laugh 'til your whole side's hurtin'
> Smile like you just go away with something
> Why? 'Cause you just got away with something
> Ever since, ever since grace got you"[10]

A Father's Rebuke and a Seed of Hope

In ***Genesis 18:12 (NLT)*** it says,

So she laughed silently to herself and said, "How could a worn-out woman like me enjoy such pleasure, especially when my master – my husband – is also so old?"

Sarah laughs to herself and then follows it with a question – *'How could this be?'* We often perceive her laughter as doubt, but is it possible that

---

[10] MercyMe, "Grace Got You," recorded 2016-2017, track 3 on *Lifer,* Fair Trade, 2017, compact disc.

Sarah's laughter planted a seed of hope, causing her to ask, "How could this be possible? I know in the natural, there is no way, but could it be?" Can you hear it now? That silent laughter, barely a whisper, saying, "Maybe it can be – I'm not quite sure how, but just maybe?"

Then, God calls her out on it and asks her why she laughs. Although she denies it, He responds as you would expect any caring father to – by lovingly showing her grace. Then He waters her seed of hope with a promise saying, *"Is anything too hard for the LORD?"* And if we read between the lines, we can hear the Father saying to Sarah:

"Go ahead, laugh, my princess. Laugh at the future. Laugh because greater is He that is in you, and nothing is impossible for me! Don't worry about the details or get bogged down in the how. Just know I AM, and your promise is on the way. So keep on laughing!"

Which Reminds Me, God's Got the Details

Many years ago, we were praying with our kids before bed, and it was my son's turn to pray. He was probably three or four at the time. Most times, he always prayed the same prayer, but this particular night he added something new. After thanking God for the day and asking God to give him a goodnight's sleep, he said the strangest thing, "And I pray for *all my details*. In Jesus' name. Amen." We laughed so hard about this at first and said to him, "What do you mean – *all your details*?" We realised he had seen something on TV while watching a kid's program. They were telling kids to draw a picture, put it in an envelope and send it to the TV station with *all their details* on the back of the envelope.

We reminisce and giggle about it now, but when we stopped to reflect on this childlike request, we realised what our son was praying was incredibly powerful – "God, please take care of *all my details*." We kept encouraging our son to pray this way because it was a beautiful way for him to lay his life before God and ask God to take care of everything.

Oh, what we as adults can learn from the heart of a child! We need to be able to lay *all our details* at Jesus's feet. He's got them. It takes complete trust, and this is what God was asking from Sarah. He didn't expect her to rationalise and figure out the exact specifics of how the promise would come to pass. He simply wanted her to take Him at His word and be able to rest in the knowledge that He would take care of all the nitty-gritty. This can be hard when you are waiting for the fulfilment of the promise. As a very rational person who always needs to understand the why and how of things down to the minutest details, this can be immensely challenging. Yet God's ways are higher than mine, so I need to learn to trust even when my mind is wrestling to fathom His ways.

God's Promise Carries Us Through the Waiting

As I have already said, when Sarah laughed at the prophecy from God, I don't believe she was totally shutting Him down. I believe her laughter was a tiny seed of hope. I believe when God heard her laugh, He said, *"I can work with that, it might be the smallest glimmer of hope, but that's all I need."*

I also love how God didn't leave her with nothing to hang onto. Instead, He gave her a promise, "Nothing is impossible for your God!" Holding onto that promise, Sarah lifted her head high and walked into her future, laughing.

Genesis 21:6 (NLT)

And Sarah declared, "God has brought me laughter. All who hear about this will laugh with me."

We, too are never alone as we wait for our dreams to become a reality. God has given us His Word filled with promise after promise to remind us He can do all things. He has poured His grace upon us though we don't deserve it and made us His very own sons and daughters. He has given us the Holy Spirit to be our Comforter, so we can press in and lean on Him for renewed strength each day. Because of this, we can face our trials and challenges with great joy and laugh at the future, like Sarah.

The Prophetic Power of Laughter

When Sarah gave birth to her son and named him Isaac, meaning '*laughter*', she was speaking prophetically over her son, and over the nation of Israel who would come from her seed. She was declaring Israel to be a nation of joy and laughter. A nation that would be distinctively different from the nations of the world because it was birthed in joy! She prophesied that Israel would carry a joy wherever it went. Joy that would impact and affect change. Joy that would be infectious and bring life into dark situations.

There is tremendous prophetic power in laughter and joy. Not just for our immediate circumstances, but for the future and the future of those around us. Our children need to see us laughing at the future. They need to see us being joyful even when things don't seem to be working out. Our colleagues need to see us laughing even when work is challenging, and the boss is doing their darnedest to make our life miserable. The world needs to see how genuine, godly joy and laughter should look. There is so much heaviness in our world, disguised in so many different forms. It can be overwhelming at times and seem like an absolute impossibility to see change. But like Sarah, we need to start laughing. We need to begin prophesying joy over our world. God can make powerful things come to pass when His children laugh.

Today you need to lift your head and laugh, God might be birthing something crazy inside you. Maybe when He first called you to that thing, you laughed. I'll admit, when God spoke to me about writing a book, that's precisely what I did. We need to remember that some of the greatest miracles have come from laughter, which have had an immense impact on our world. I don't know about you, but I think our world could certainly do with more miracles. So when God puts a crazy dream in your heart, go right on ahead and laugh! Bring forth laughter as He makes your dreams come true and see the world changed for His glory.

1 Peter 1:5-9 (TPT)

Through our faith, the mighty power of God constantly guards us until our full salvation is ready to be revealed in the last time. ***May the thought of this cause you to jump for joy,*** *even though lately you've had to put up with the grief of many trials. But these only reveal the sterling core of your faith, which is far more valuable than gold that perishes, for even gold is refined by fire. Your authentic faith will result in even more praise, glory, and honor when Jesus the Anointed One is revealed. You love him passionately although you did not see him,* ***but through believing in him you are saturated with an ecstatic joy,*** *indescribably sublime and immersed in glory. For you are reaping the harvest of your faith – the full salvation promised you – your souls' victory.*

Conclusion

This Wondrous Life!

Psalm 121 (NIV)
A song of ascents.

*1 "I lift up my eyes to the mountains –
where does my help come from?
2 My help comes from the Lord,
the Maker of Heaven and earth.
3 He will not let your foot slip –
he who watches over you will not slumber;
4 indeed, he who watches over Israel
will neither slumber nor sleep.
5 The Lord watches over you –
the Lord is your shade at your right hand;
6 the sun will not harm you by day,
nor the moon by night.*

> *7 The Lord will keep you from all harm –*
> *he will watch over your life;*
> *8 the Lord will watch over your coming and going*
> *both now and forevermore."*

So when all is said and done, what is *'This Wondrous Life'* all about? It's about a life lived with Father God, Jesus, and the Holy Spirit at the very centre. I think Psalm 121 beautifully depicts this. In the Hebrew tradition, Psalm 121 was often read before the beginning of a journey. It is typically known as a Psalm of protection. For me, it's a life Psalm because life is a journey. Each and every day is a part of that journey. As Christians, our journey is Heaven bound, and knowing that my God is with me every step of the way is paramount to this.

In my home, I have this Psalm written in Hebrew. It sits in our foyer as a prayer and constant reminder to our family, that first and foremost, God is the centre of our lives. It is Him who we look to in all things. Secondly, it is a banner over each one of us, declaring our Lord is with us in all things, the day and the night, when we rise and when we sleep, when we go and when we come.

In ***John 10:10 (NIV)*** it says:

The thief comes only to steal and kill and destroy; I have come that they may have life, and have it to the full.

Jesus told us that He came so that we might have life and life to the full. The fullness of life doesn't mean everything will always be perfect. The fullness of life is a journey, much like the Psalmist refers to in Psalm 121. There will be mountains to climb and valleys to walk through. There will be straight, flat roads and ones that weave and wind. Some will be smooth and easy to traverse. Others will be rough underfoot. But regardless, the journey of life will be full because Jesus will be right there by our sides. Perhaps the apostle Paul says it best when he writes to the church in Philippi in ***Philippians 4:11-13 (NIV)***:

I am not saying this because I am in need, for I have learned to be content whatever the circumstances. I know what it is to be in need, and I know what it is to have plenty. I have learned the secret of being content in any and every situation, whether well fed or hungry, whether living in plenty or in want. I can do all this through him who gives me strength.

Paul was not only referring to the positives when he wrote these words. He was in very dire circumstances when he wrote this letter to the Philippians. Paul was in prison, facing a very uncertain future. Yet despite this, he could still write these famous words, *"I can do all this through him who gives me the strength."*

What did he mean by *'all this*? What did he mean when he said, *'I have learned the secret of being content in any and every situation?'*

Jesus.

Jesus was the key. Jesus was central to Paul's remarkable statement of faith.

The challenge for us today in embracing *'This Wondrous Life'* is to know Christ as our central treasure. He is our complete satisfaction in all things. In Him, we can discover, understand and live out tremendous contentment. In Him, we put our hope and believe for greater things to come. In Him, we dream. In Him, we step out in faith. In Him, we keep moving forward. In Him, we journey toward eternity. And in Him, we can boldly declare, *"I can do all this through Him who gives me strength."*

One day I will meet my Maker face to face. The One who I have been betrothed to since I was a young girl. The One who has held my heart and my hand throughout my life. I have pondered that moment thousands of times. Every time so beautiful, it takes my breath away. When I get there, I know all of Heaven will be anticipating my arrival. I don't view my journey on earth as just getting by until I finally make it to Heaven. No! This life is only the beginning. That's why I can smile at the future and live this life in all its fullness. Fullness doesn't begin when I arrive in Heaven. Full living starts now. And the moment when I see His face will be the continuation of *'This Wondrous Life'*.

Standing at the threshold of Your holy place
All of Heaven whispers, "She's arrived"
You take my hand, twirl me around
Draw me close, whisper that I'm found
It's the moment I've been waiting for—all my life
My first dance in Heaven

Just the King and I

Bibliography

Andrews, Stephen J., Bergen, Robert D., and Anders, Max. *1, 2 Samuel*: Holman Old Testament Commentary. Nashville, Tennessee: B&H Publishing Group, 2009.

Chapman, Stephen B. *1 Samuel as Christian Scripture*: A Theological Commentary. Grand Rapids, Michigan: William B. Eerdmans Publishing, 2016.

Holy Bible. New International Version. Grand Rapids, Michigan: Zondervan Publishing House, 2011.

Holy Bible. New Living Translation. Carol Stream, Illinois: Tyndale House, 2015.

Ligertwood, Brooke. Hillsong Worship. "Desert Song." Recorded March 2008. Track 3 on *This Is Our God*. Hillsong Publishing, 2007, compact disc.

MercyMe. "Grace Got Me." Recorded 2016-2017. Track 3 on *Lifer*. Fair Trade, 2017, compact disc.

The Holy Bible. New King James Version. Thomas Nelson, 1982.

The Passion Translation Second Edition. Broad Street Publishing, 2018.

The Voice Bible. Thomas Nelson, 2012.

Wonder Woman. Directed by Patty Jenkins. DC Films, 2017. Motion Picture. Warner Bros. Pictures, 2017.

Yoon, Carol Kaesong Yoon, "Clues to Redwoods' Mighty Growth Emerge in Fog," *New York Times,* Nov. 24, 1998.

Youngblood, Ronald F., Longman III,Tremper., and Garland, David E. *1 and 2 Samuel*: The Expositor's Bible Commentary. Grand Rapids, Michigan: Harper Collins Christian Publishing, 2017.

About the Author

Andrina Rijken is passionate about being an extravagant worshiper and learning all she can about the Word of God. She desires to inspire others to experience a deep and wonderful relationship with their Saviour Jesus in their everyday lives. Growing up as a pastor's daughter, she has been involved in many different aspects of ministry, including church planting, pastoral care, worship, youth work and children's ministry. Andrina lives in Brisbane, Australia, with her husband and children. She has a Bachelor of Speech Pathology with over twenty years of experience in this field. Andrina is currently completing a Master of Arts majoring in Christian Studies at Alphacrucis College.

www.ingramcontent.com/pod-product-compliance
Lightning Source LLC
Chambersburg PA
CBHW070500100426
42743CB00010B/1693